Attempts

Attempts

Essays on Fitness, Health, Longevity and Easy Strength

Dan John

On Target Publications
Aptos, California

Attempts
Essays on Fitness, Health, Longevity and Easy Strength

Dan John

Original Strength images on pages 209–211 compliments of Tim Anderson

ISBN-13: 978-1-931046-12-1 (paperback)
ISBN-13: 978-1-931046-06-0 (epub)
First printing July 2020

On Target Publications
P O Box 1335
Aptos, California 95001 USA
otpbooks.com

Library of Congress Control Number: 2020941003

Also by Dan John

40 Years with a Whistle

Now What?

The Hardstyle Kettlebell Challenge

Can You Go?

Before We Go

Intervention

Never Let Go

Mass Made Simple

From Dad to Grad

Easy Strength
(with Pavel Tsatsouline)

Fat Loss Happens on Monday
(with Josh Hillis)

To my brother, Phil

His death was tragedy. My memories are comedy.

His life story can be summed simply: He showed up.

To my other brothers who died on that August day.

Contents

Building the Foundation

Life Lessons—Some Tough, All True

Some Big Ideas about Training... and Life

Appendices

Building the Foundation

On Essays, or, How I wrote this Work

Michel de Montaigne wrote his series of books, *Essays*, around the time the Spanish Armada was winging its way toward England. Shakespeare and Cervantes could have had tea with Montaigne, and some think Shakespeare used Montaigne's writings as inspiration (that tea party would make a fine play). As part of my Great Books experience, I read and discussed the essays at length about 400 years later.

I loved reading his work and I still love this selection we find in *On Drunkenness*:

> *"Plato forbids children wine till 18 years of age, and to get drunk till 40; but, after 40, gives them leave to please themselves, and to mix a little liberally in their feasts the influence of Dionysos, that good deity who restores to younger men their gayety, and to old men their youth; who mollifies the passions of the soul, as iron is softened by fire; and in his laws allows such merry meetings, provided they have a discreet chief to govern and keep them in order, as good and of great utility; drunkenness being, he says, a true and certain trial of every one's nature, and, withal, fit to inspire old men with mettle to divert themselves in dancing and music; things of great use, and that they dare not attempt when sober."*

"Dare not attempt when sober."

It made me laugh out loud when I first read this line and I continue to admire his style.

Essays comes from the French word *essais* which means "attempts." I enjoyed reading this open-ended style of asking a question (rhetorical) and then diving into the topic. The route from asking the question to discovering some insights might take a few pages of writing or months (or years… or decades!) of rewriting and rethinking.

My friend, Jim, says that his best insights come from mowing the lawn, as the act of walking back and forth, back and forth, seems to turn off his brain and, oddly, allows him to think.

I think by writing.

Generally, I strive to *solve* problems, as I think any idiot can find problems. I may start off by writing the story of the problem—either how I heard about the issue, or how I had run into one of life's roadblocks. I strive for three solutions because that seems to make my mind most comfortable. I might add a story or two here and there, and I try my best to be prudent about the expenses, cost-to-benefit ratio and reality of my solution.

That last part is crucial: All too often hoping for a miracle or wishing for more money or a bigger budget isn't going to prod the reader to following a vision.

That's why I explore things until something simple pops up and leads back on the journey to mastery.

I hope you enjoy my "attempts."

What I Mean by Fitness, Health, Longevity and Performance

"What do YOU mean by that?"

I get asked a fair amount of questions at parties. If you train people, party goers want you to sum nearly 60 years of experience in fitness and training in one sentence… then, they argue with you about something they read on the internet.

Since I also teach religious studies, I get hammered by additional questions about ghosts, dead aunts communicating across the void and questions about aliens. I used to answer as best I could, but then I discovered the key:

The follow-up question.

"Dan, I'm not religious, but I'm VERY spiritual."

"What do YOU mean by that?"

"Oh, I read my horoscope daily."

Ah.

When I get asked about the direction of the wide, wide world of fitness, I ask a question first:

"What do YOU mean by that?"

"Mean by what?"

Let me help. Let's just look at a few words that come to mind when the word "fitness" gets used:

Health

Longevity

Nutrition (Diet)

Fitness

Performance

You see, these five words are not redundant. Let me say that again. They are not redundant (I hope some of you get that joke).

The problem we have is this: Since many people link those words under one hat, all sorts of problems come up.

I use Phil Maffetone's definition of health: the optimal interplay of the human organs. You can be big, weak, small, bony, tired and anything else you can dream up and still be healthy.

Healthy is lack of disease. I always think "dis-ease" would be a better way to write the word because it's literally the lack of ease in moving blood, waste materials, food and yourself around the body that's the problem somewhere.

Health is discovered through blood profiles, some medical machine's magic report and a visit to someone who went to medical, dental or optometry school. No matter how many crystals you dangle over my chest, you won't find skin cancer on my leg with this method.

The future of health does NOT look good. Obesity is statistically growing so fast that researchers have a hard time keeping up with how to make the charts work to explain how fast obesity is growing. Obesity leads to a cascade of health issues and "eat less, move more" is basically right, but it can't work alone.

That's health. Let's talk about longevity.

I can easily answer questions about longevity: Don't die.

You're welcome.

If you don't have health, you might not want longevity, but that's a personal issue. I love reading and studying about longevity because it's something my family doesn't seem to have.

Bill Gifford's book *Spring Chicken* does a wonderful job outlining the various issues with longevity. As we boil down the essentials, we find nothing new under the sun:

> *Exercise—maybe as little as 100 minutes a week*
>
> *Fast—at some level, religious traditions all have this concept*
>
> *Drink more coffee and wine. Yes, true—but here's the thing; these are two "social" beverages and perhaps the connections you have are more important than whether or not you take some exotic herb.*

Mostly, it helps to be from long-living families… and don't die.

For me, it's always about the quality over quantity of life, but I also think the two concepts intertwine.

I can tell you what most people think about nutrition and diet: rabbit food and starvation.

I went to a conference in Norway and one thing the nutrition presenters hammered down on the audience talk after talk:

Our brains are NOT wired to deal with the noise.

We expect feast and famine. Yet, advertisers hit us daily with literally hours of fast food and restaurant promotions. When you get to the café, you see dozens of breakfast selections. When you get to the store, you find a vast variety of different kinds of milk.

Decisions. Decisions. Decisions.

Recently, two friends visited from Scotland. We had a wonderful discussion about orange juice. Yes, orange juice.

In Scotland, you buy OJ.

Here in the States? Well, you'd better prepare for the options: low pulp, no pulp, extra pulp. Vitamin D added. Calcium added.

It's like going into a chain coffee shop and asking for a damn cup of coffee. They respond with a bunch of Italian-sounding names, various languages for the drink size, and a price tag equivalent of buying a coffee maker for yourself... and a pound of coffee.

You can eat poorly and still look good. My NFL coaching friends all have stories of the players' cars being loaded with fast food bags in the back seats. At 22 years of age and 60 hours of training each week, they can probably deal with that mess. If you want to eat poorly and look good, be 22 and train about 60 hours a week.

The rest of us just seem to be getting fatter.

The best thing we can do for the future is CUT BACK on choices. Get cartoon characters off of breakfast cereal, simplify shopping and stop allowing companies to fill your decision matrix with ever more enticing food.

No, that won't happen. Capitalism defines democracy for most people, and the food industry studies the same things nutritionists study, except they flip the orientation from health to profit.

That's just the way it is and will continue to be. The battle against the obesity epidemic is uphill, and we're rolling down quickly.

So. Less choice means less fat (around the waist). Let's move on.

I use Darwin's definition of fitness: the ability to do a task.

That's it.

I don't want to hear that a marathoner is "The Fittest Person on the Planet." Or, really, anyone you can fill in the blank with whatever sport or thing you want.

If a 103-year-old man becomes a father (Props! In all ways of the word!), he is fit for fatherhood. He might not be able to do all the tasks of a dad, but he is fit for the task of being a father.

And, that's it.

The future of the fitness world will continue to stumble around this concept. "Fit for what?" must be part of your language.

If you want to be an elite thrower, you can't also compete in the marathon. NFL offensive linemen would not make good Kentucky Derby jockeys, even if they think they might look good in a jockey outfit.

Performance? That's when they call your name and you step under the lights and compete.

I coach people to be better in these moments. One of the ways I do it is with clarity of health, longevity, diet and fitness. There are times when your performance might—perhaps just in the short run—impact your health. Cutting weight to make a competitive weight class is also fraught with issues. Just remember; it's a short-term thing, NOT a lifestyle.

What's the future of this field?

In my opinion, we'll follow the model of fast food and junk food. The future of fitness will be crowded with many conflicting choices that make lots of claims and promises.

Most of us will fail, flounder and flop. And… our bank accounts will have a lot less in them.

That's not the rosiest picture I've ever painted.

Attempts

Save yourself now. Focus on the fundamentals, the basics.

Eat like an adult. Have a social life. Go for a walk. Do fundamental human movements and master them. Keep coming back.

And, soon, at a party, someone will ask how you keep so fit. You may want to follow up with, "What do YOU mean by that?"

My Three Essential Coaching and Life "Truths"

Before I get too far here, you have to understand that the following could all change. I've been practicing these basic three truths since I first touched a barbell in 1965 and they've kept me happy, healthy and hearty ever since.

Yet, I could be wrong. I have to keep that window open. My brother, Gary, once joked, "I've been wrong before. It was 1962. I thought I was wrong. Later, it turns out I was right, but I still count that one time."

As we go through the list, don't expect to have your hair blown off or see colors get brighter. It's simple stuff.

Let's get the list out there:

1. Invest wisely in asymmetrical risks.

2. Embrace the obvious.

3. Respect the process and the results will take care of themselves.

When I break this down, it's going to be fairly simple to adopt this system:

ASYMMETRICAL RISKS

What's the worst that can happen?

EMBRACE THE OBVIOUS

What's the obvious solution?

RESPECT THE PROCESS

Oddly, little and often over the long haul worked!

Let's look at each one.

Invest wisely in asymmetrical risks.

I live in a place where many of my neighbors are proud to have a two-year supply of food. That's a nice cache of food to have to overcome practically any issue. Of course, when the COVID-19 crisis hit, most of them also rushed to the store to hoard food and toilet paper.

I'm just guessing, but if you're trying to survive for two years, food and toilet paper might be on your prep list.

I'm not sure if my neighbors really had the two-year supply of food, but storing that much stuff is going to be tough. Keeping it all fresh, rotated and bug or rodent safe takes a lot of effort.

Here's the thing, though: The idea is right! I buy these $20 backpacks that have a three-day supply of water, food and basic supplies for four people. I have one in every car we own, and I make sure my daughters have them in their cars too.

I live in a desert (technically, "high" desert), and there are many places you simply don't want to break down and get stuck in your vehicle. These backpacks are 20 dollars. If my daughter and grandkids get stranded on a blistering hot day on some back road, how much is that backpack worth?

For me, it's priceless.

During the 2002 Olympics when I was an administrator, I had to go to lots of disaster preparation courses. Nothing happened, yet for those of us who remembered the events of 9/11, we were all worried.

The best thing about these courses was learning the simple steps we can take to maintain our safety and security without losing our minds. Let me give you some ideas from the material.

- The big good news: If you can survive in your home for three days, statistically, the worst of most disasters will be behind you.

- Keep old sweats or warm gear in your car. The funny part about this was when the woman told us it's very common to arrive at a fire and discover the homeowners need something to wear… a LOT of people sleep in the nude. You might as well toss in some extra shoes, gloves and a hat. If not for you, do it for a more modest friend or neighbor.

- Most people don't need to store water. The hot water heater has refreshed water and plenty of it.

- If something terrible does happen, the woman told us that a mere 90 miles will get us away from the epicenter of most disasters. She then told us to count overpasses on the way home and remind yourself that many might be down. Investing in a sturdy bicycle (and that $20 backpack) will get you clear of most events.

- With modern phones, much of the problems of finding people will be easier, but taking a few minutes annually to review a link-up plan is worth the time.

Almost all of these are simple. Of course, the doing is far more important than the knowing. These courses were a doctorate in investing wisely in asymmetrical risks.

A few years ago, with no timeouts and only 11 seconds left on the clock, the Navy football team rushed their field goal team out and made the kick. The sporting world was shocked by this show of efficiency, but the coach pointed out that they had practiced this time and again because getting those three points makes or breaks a game. That's a wise investment of practice time.

I simplify this concept in workshops down another rung: What's the worst that can happen?

I then describe a few events in my career:

- If you're coaching 92 adolescent boys in full American football gear, what's the worst that can happen?

- If you're coaching 62 14-year-old boys in the weight room—by yourself—what's the worst that can happen?

- After the movie *300* came out and a lot of young boys wanted to play with javelins, what's the worst that can happen?

Yeah. A LOT of worsts can happen when you coach scholastic athletes. The wise coach will have walls, barriers, chains, guard dogs, sharks and zombies protecting against the worst possibilities.

When I travel, I pack for great weather... and horrible weather. I get sick sometimes, so I carry a variety of medicines. I always bring lots of extra coffee because no hotel has enough for me.

What's the worst that can happen when I travel? I have pictures of my passport in a file online. I have family members and a friend with all the information I might need on their phones. I'm one text message from a lot of important travel information. Why? Because losing your passport might be the worst thing MOST of us ever deal with in travel.

True, there are kidnappings, terror, war, typhoons and tsunamis. I have some things in my luggage bag that can deal with some of this too.

What's the worst?

Think it through, then see if you can take some small, simple steps to alleviate those worsts. Often, this practice makes the best better, too.

Embrace the obvious.

It's pretty obvious, yes. That doesn't make it any less valuable.

I've turned this into a cliché in my workshops and podcasts. I say this A LOT:

> Runners run.
>
> Throwers throw.
>
> Hurdlers hurdle.
>
> Sprinters sprint.
>
> Swimmers swim.

You get the point. I often add this:

> To get stronger, lift weights.
>
> For recovery, sleep.
>
> For hydration, drink water.

Oddly, this makes people laugh.

I laugh, too, because it's, well, obvious.

Embrace this.

When faced with a problem, a simple way to begin is this: What's the obvious solution?

No matter what sport, game, occupation or journey you embark upon, focusing on the obvious will help. Certainly, you need to deal with the smaller details, but master the obvious first.

I have a book on lightweight hiking that sums up trekking as:

A sleep system

A food system

A carrying system

Clearly, there's much more to this adventure than these three things, but if you embark on the Appalachian Trail and ignore one of these keys you're going to face problems very soon.

John Heisman summed American football in 1931 with these three points:

Block

Tackle

Fall on the ball (today, we'd call this "ball control")

Mastery of these three things almost ensures victory (of course, things can still happen).

In *Now What?*, I discussed the "five whys" of reviewing missed tackles in games. Here's the thing: If you make every tackle, you might never lose.

And, that's obvious.

Embrace it. Fall in love with it. When I asked Coach Ralph Maughan the secret of throwing the discus far, he told me, "Throw the discus four days a week. Lift weights three days a week... for the next eight years."

I expected a secret. He told me something obvious. He was right. The greatest secret I know in every field of life is always obvious.

Embrace the obvious.

Respect the process.

I struggled when I first became a head football coach. I couldn't decide whether to coach like Vince Lombardi or Knute Rockne or (submit the name of any famous coach). That was the issue, among many, at first.

I wasn't following my own vision, my own path.

I finally gained ground when I realized coaching like a made-for-TV movie wasn't helping. I realized this when our team was winless. We were winless, and I kept trying to win games.

That's odd to say; it's odd to write. I was hoping that a half-time speech or pregame oratory would propel my young squad to victory. I was focusing on the results and, frankly, we weren't good enough to win. On pure talent, the other teams were better.

I still wanted to win (obviously… notice how that word, "obvious," keeps showing up). I began looking at how we were losing games. It was coming down to a few things. We often only had nine people on special teams—you should have 11—and we were poor at executing situational plays.

I then decided it was time to spend practice on the things that were killing us in games and invented a drill called "third and 15." The offense would try to get a first down on one play. If they succeeded, we did another "third and 15." If they didn't, I sent out the punt team and we punted to our scout team.

I quickly realized that the same boy who forgot he was on the punt team continued to forget he was on the punt team. We subbed him for another athlete, and the problem vanished.

I began scheduling practice around the keys to winning (block, tackle and fall on the ball) and game-time problems and solutions. I ignored winning, and became more cerebral about taking advantage of the small wins in the game.

We finished by winning our last five games, with several being exciting overtime victories.

The fans got their money's worth. Of course, at this level of play, the games are free.

But still… they got their money's worth!

Coach Maughan told me that greatness in the discus would take eight years. He summed track and field, and most of life, with this phrase:

"Little and often over the long haul."

I say it a lot. I don't say it often enough.

Here's the thing: You can't control the results!

You may save money for decades, and see it get wiped out overnight in a crazy stock market. But saving money is ALWAYS a good thing. Drinking water, eating veggies, wearing a seatbelt and flossing your teeth is always going to be good advice.

You still may end up with "issues," even if you floss your teeth twice a day. But you did what you could do.

Respect the process. Do the things that nudge you toward success. Earl Nightingale reminded us that, "Success is the progressive realization of a worthy goal or ideal." We can talk about "worthy" any time you like.

"Progressive realization" doesn't mean you get the gold medal, world record or championship ring. Others want that too, and they might simply be better. At birth, some people win the genetic roulette. Height and speed seem to be a gift from the gods.

Hard work can overcome a lot, but when talent mixes discipline and hard work, it's a world-beater.

Respect the process. Do the basics. Do the fundamentals.

And do them often.

For a long time.

On January and the Importance of Looking Back

Whether the month of January was named after Janus or Juno might still be an issue in the wings of the Latin department of your local school, but many of us accept that Janus makes a great symbol for the month of January.

Janus has two heads, one looking forward and the other looking backward. January 1st is the standard date most people begin their New Year's Resolutions and somewhere in the next day or two, most people ignore them.

For personal trainers and coaches alike, the first of the year is a good time for business and a bad time for success. We find in Janus a good way to begin our year:

Look backward first!

When I'm working with athletes or clients, I want to get to know them a bit. Certainly, we'll do physical assessments and highlight past injuries, surgeries and illnesses, but it's important to know the path each new client has taken to get to you.

Forty-plus years of filling yourself with soft drinks and sweets and extra desserts while steadfastly battling back any urge to exercise might also be something we want to discuss in passing.

I wrote an article years ago with the idea that NEXT year's resolution should be to weigh one pound less on the first of January than you do this year. The article got slammed by many readers. This obviously wasn't hardcore enough, nor sexy or glitzy. But, as I warned one person, "Gentle reader, get back to me next January 1st."

Perhaps the internet has been down—I never got a response.

Nor do I expect it.

Before we march forward, we need to check in on how and what we have been doing for the past few decades.

Janus is a good symbol for goal setting: Look forward, yes, but remember how you got here.

It's Not Where You Start, It's Where You Finish

We have a family mission statement: Make a difference. I run this through my mind on every decision and every time I review this occasionally horrible question: "Was that worth it?" If it made a difference to someone somewhere… the answer is, "YES!"

We also have a family motto: It's not where you start, it's where you finish. My wife, Tiffini, and I both grew up in financially challenged families, unusual stressors (having brothers fight in war impacted much of my youth) and the usual issues that plague teens and young adults.

My daughters fiercely embrace this motto. They were both undersized throwers and struggled, as I did, with bigger athletes winning the meets in the early years. Later, both mastered the advanced techniques and defeated these same athletes at the state meet.

People ask about my athletic career, and I love to point out that my first discus throw went two feet BEHIND the ring. At my first high school meet, I threw 72 feet… at my last one, I threw 170.

It's not where you start.

When I think back to 1985, I remember sitting in a basement apartment, listing my debts. I was sleeping in a foldout bed and my car was being towed away as it would never drive again.

I owed $600, and I was still sick from a bug from the Middle East.

I wrote down some options. I made a plan. I thought about what I wanted in life.

I moved forward when sometimes getting up out of bed was a chore. I look back and realize, as I stare out at my home and family, that goal setting is simply understanding that we're going from "here to there."

It's where you finish.

People love to set goals on January 1st. As I said, I now tell people to strive to weigh one pound less on the following New Year's Day. People laugh at that. The following year, usually after not training or eating well for 360 days (they did follow an exercise and nutritional program for the first five days of the new year), the scale groans back a new 10 pounds over last year.

So, we start again. Ideally, this time, we'll finish.

It's a great life lesson. And, like all great life lessons, it's the journey. I love to quote Cervantes: "It's the road, not the inn."

It's not where you start, it's where you finish.

"A," "Not A" Goals

One of the biggest mistakes I made in my career is listening to people. Don't take that wrong: I actually listen to people.

And... that's often wrong.

When I work with athletes, I ask very few questions. "How far do you throw?" "What's your time?"

You see, with athletes, they are, literally, their numbers. Throw the discus 190 feet and you're a 190-foot thrower. To get to 200 feet, we walk a very narrow plank from 190 to 200. If we do something innovative and brilliant and throw 150... well...

We were wrong!

With most people, it's not so easy. They don't have those nice numbers. In fact, most people will have goal after goal after goal.

> *"I want to lose weight. I want to shrink my waistline. I want to exercise more. I want to eat right."*

And, at least in my experience, most people barely exit the room before they undo the bulk of those statements.

You see, most people are trying very simply to tell us something when it comes to goal setting:

You see *this* person here?

Yeah, that's not me.

Me? I'm young and beautiful and turn heads when I walk. Give me two weeks and I will be 18 years old again.

"Aren't you 79?"

Yeah… well.

This often gets a chuckle at workshops, but then a reality cloud covers the room.

"Yeah, no one knows this… but this is not me either."

Before you even attempt to set goals with most people, you have to discuss the idea of "not me."

This isn't witchcraft or wizardly; it's a truth. Like Socrates' unexamined life, we also need to examine our relationship with the body, the "me" we inhabit.

Me? I need to do the same!

Forthteller, not a Fortuneteller

I took a Hebrew scriptures course over a four-week period back in the mid-1980s. There was a lot of reading, and a lot of work. I was the lone student on the last night.

I like to finish things. The upside of being the only student is that the instructor had time to help me dig deeply into the material. That last night, I used the word "prophet" in the traditional sense—one who speaks for another.

The instructor smiled and said:

"Let's add a little bit to that."

I was told that the key to understand not only biblical prophets but ALL prophets is to understand they aren't telling us the future. They don't roll sticks, bones or shells to bedazzle us with our journey to meeting a tall, dark, handsome man. Rather, they are forthtellers.

Prophets, and those who work in the prophetic world, are those people who tell you the truth. They speak forth. The true prophet reminds us that if we continue doing this or that, we can't be surprised where we end up.

We're the sum of our past decisions. True, things happen, but as Victor Frankl reminded us, "Everything can be taken from a man but one thing: the last of the human freedoms—to choose one's attitude in any given set of circumstances, to choose one's own way."

I know, bad things happen. I know. But we still have the ability to choose our attitude about it.

Coaches, teachers, parents and family often fill the role of forthteller. Listen, that beer and pizza diet of freshman college girls is NOT optimal. I bumped into a former student a while ago, and the student asked if I recognized him.

"Of course, of course."

Honestly, I recognized only a third of him. He didn't pay attention in high school when we discussed food, exercise and recovery and, well, it showed.

I've had adults tell me they wish they had never started smoking. Honestly, not ONE person or ad or health class ever warned you about smoking? If you fought in World War II and were given free cigarettes and worried about the Nazis, I get it, but…

Here's the bottom line: From the heart, you know what to do when it comes to food (eat like an adult), exercise (yeah… do some) and sleep (go to bed!). There are few surprises in life. To be successful in school, show up, listen and earnestly work on your assignments.

We could go on forever here.

Sometimes the coach, trainer, author, parent, friend or family member will give you some forthtelling.

Listen to it. Embrace it. The forthtellers often predict the future.

Tony Robbins ... Pain and Pleasure

I was sitting in a crappy hotel in Fort Collins, Colorado. This was the place the meet director told the athletes to book. I hoped it was cheap, as the walls were basically cardboard and I could smell the traffic coming under the huge gap in the door.

There weren't any food places nearby. Note, I didn't say restaurants or cafes as that would be too much to ask. But I did find a convenience store with wrapped sandwiches. I'm sure they were as fresh as the coffee that had enough oil to take care of a truck engine.

I felt sorry for myself sitting in that room. The weigh master—the person who measures track and field implements—had been trained for courtesy by the TSA; he bitched about my discus for some reason that escapes me. I was eating crappy, feeling alone and nervous about the Nationals the next day.

There was literally nothing on the TV other than infomercials. I stopped on one: *Tony Robbins' Get the Edge*. Just watching the show, besides buying it the following Monday, changed my perception. As he often states, in an INSTANT, I changed my mental matrix on what was "happening to me" and took solid ownership. The next day, I broke the American record in the weight pentathlon.

We can't ignore that I'd trained for this for years, and we can't skip that I know how to turn on my arousal during competition.

This is all true; but I also know that my mind switched on while listening Robbins. Soon, I was following his directions exactly as he outlined.

I know how to goal set. As a track and field athlete, just striving to go farther or faster is a form of goal setting. But how do we translate this to most people?

Robbins' insight of using pain and pleasure opened the door for me. Here's what most people think:

> If I get my goal, I'll be happy.

> If I don't get my goal, I'll be sad.

It's simply not true: Pain and pleasure are something we need to understand better.

Is there pleasure in NOT getting my goal?

> Yes.

Is there pain in GETTING my goal?

> Yes.

This needs to be discussed.

THE PLEASURE OF NOT ACHIEVING A GOAL

Most New Year's Resolutions don't survive the college football bowl games on January 1st. The person who swore off booze and snacking often has belly full of both by halftime of the Rose Bowl.

Yet, just hours before, this same person was the epitome of discipline... the idol of the society of self-sacrifice! It's not something most people think about, but it's a truth:

There's a LOT more pleasure in NOT achieving a goal. It's obvious when you think about it.

If I tell you you're going to live on starvation rations for a month and train 12 hours a day, you know there's going to be a lot of pain. Lots.

Snacking is pleasurable. Candy tastes good. Pie makes me happy. Cake reminds me of weddings and birthdays. Sitting down and watching comedies is fun.

Not sticking to the goal is often very nice. Extremely nice… so nice that this is what most people do.

When I help someone undertake a four-year commitment, like to the Olympics, I ask them as clearly as I can to respond honestly:

If you don't make the team or get a medal, what joy or happiness will come from this?

Universally, the answer is, "Nothing."

But, is this true?

It's my job to tell the stories. Lovers get very tired of your travel and training schedules. Being in love and loved is pleasurable. NOT sitting in crappy hotels and crappy airports is a lot better than sitting in them.

This is the toughest one: Acknowledging on day one of a four-year voyage that you could be actively seeking things that are more fun and joyous than strict meals and strict training.

Growing up, we all knew dozens of people who wanted to be dancers, singers, artists and athletes who discovered much more fun things to do with their time.

Here's the key: Talking openly and honestly about the wonderful things in life that conspire to cut off the knees of our brilliant goal setting seems to be a positive force in later keeping people on track.

It's like warning a friend about a dangerous intersection and, maybe years later, being thanked for "saving my life" as he slowed coming to it.

That seems to be how our brains work; with a bit of warning, we seem to be more alert to the upcoming dangers.

Before you give up everything, be sure you think about what you will be giving up.

THE PAIN OF ACHIEVING A GOAL

Wait, what? The pain of achieving a goal?

But, dear counselor and friend, this is my goal! Won't all my dreams come true when I win the prize or get the leading role?

Yes. Yes. ONE of your dreams will come true.

But, almost invariably, many other things you want will NOT happen. If you choose to get married and raise a wonderful family (and good for you) right out of high school, you might find your dreams of being a ballerina or pro baseball player shot down. If you choose the route of the deep dive into athletics or athletic professions (dancing or special forces... as broad examples), you might find things like weekends, parties and comfort will elude you for a long time.

When you get your goal, almost instantly someone will ask about next year... or the next contest or the next show. When you achieve your goal, you'll rise above a certain level and meet a whole new cadre of people who are just as focused and just as determined to grab the next gold ring.

Frankly... it's a pain.

Yes, it seems odd to have people think about the pain of goal achievement. But it helps.

It helps to think that, "I might have to give up all of this (and make both hands nice and wide as you explain this), but once I have my goal, I can revisit all these other things."

I gave up years of nightlife and partying—I might be the only adult in the late 1970s to have never been to a disco—for my goals and dreams. Now I can certainly catch up to all the Bee Gees and Donna Summer tunes each and every day of my life.

I don't. But, I could.

That's a good thing to remember in goal setting: I could do a million things.

But. I choose to do this. And I accept the fact that I will be giving up a million things I could be doing.

Choose wisely.

THE PAIN OF NOT ACHIEVING A GOAL

This one is obvious, right?

Except it's not.

Using the lever of this pain in not achieving a goal seems to be the best coaching tool I can use for motivation.

Years ago in a small café in Orlando, I sat down with a young man who had big dreams. I learned a lot about coaching in sharing this pain and pleasure assignment with him.

This was the area—the pain of not achieving a goal—that brought fire and fury out of him over breakfast. His pancakes got cold while he went on a long rant about one thing:

His ex-girlfriend would be right!

What drove him on was the pain of failure. What made him roll out of bed and eat eggs and veggies, then lift, then work, then come home and train was the painful memory of his ex-girlfriend calling him out for failing at other attempts toward greatness.

The hatred of failure is an amazing lever to push people in the right direction.

In this case, it was relatively easy to motivate this young man. Every time things would get in the way of his training or monastic existence, I merely pushed a lever:

"Ah, then. Okay. I'm fine with it. It just burns me up to think your ex-girlfriend is going to be right."

Yep. I'm a jerk.

Even after he'd heard this several times (not too often, to his credit), he KNEW it was coming and would interject an, "I know what's coming."

And it didn't matter. The lever was real and it worked every time.

Pain is an amazing lever; Archimedes argued he could move the earth with the right lever, and Coach Archimedes was right about goal setting.

Championships are usually built on the foundation of failure. Pain teaches. Pain transforms.

Please don't think this is healthy, happy or wonderful. It is, however, a truth.

Learning to lever the fear of failure makes me feel horrible.

In my defense, I'm saving the athlete (or client) some horrible long-term pain.

I'm not a hero; it's a truth of goal setting.

THE PLEASURE OF ACHIEVING A GOAL

Finally!

This will once again come off as a bit strange, but very often people answer this question, "What are the pleasures with achieving this goal?" with something like:

It would be cool.

It would be nice.

"Nice" and "cool" are great for early evenings, but these responses don't fire up the imagination. I have often wished to go back in time and tell my little self that all the sacrifices and sufferings (physical, mental and emotional) pale in the face of the highlights and accomplishments.

Wearing the school or national colors is so much greater than one might think. Having cameras in your face during the flush of victory is worth every rep of every squat. The "white moments of victory," as Yuri Vaslov coined the term, is worth facing the edge of the blade every day.

Wouldn't that be cool and nice?

That's it… right there: Most people don't really think through the wonders and pleasures of achieving a goal. It's not just wearing a swimsuit; it's strutting in a swimsuit. It's being invited to speak at corporations about your journey. It's first class, limos and priority seating. It's getting your name yelled out at you in foreign countries.

Years after achieving your goals, you might find yourself cleaning out the garage or doing some other task and discover yourself secretly smiling.

Yeah, I did that.

I try to get people to fill up that bucket of "pre-memories" of goal achievement. I want for them richer, deeper and vivid memories of joy, happiness and glory. I want the achievement of the goal so luscious, so passionate and so juicy that any and all obstacles, pain and agony are secondary to the amazing life of a goal achiever.

Fill the pot of "the pleasure of achieving a goal" as richly as you can. There are days ahead, like the old poem about Noah on the Ark, "the days are long, Lord, the days are long," but there is treasure at the end.

Seek the treasure.

The Dublin Joke

One of my favorite goal-setting points involves an oft-told joke.

A man is driving around the countryside of Ireland. He's lost and can't figure out the various twists and turns of many of the counties of Ireland.

He pulls over and asks a man a simple question:

"Pardon me, how to you get to Dublin?"

The man answers:

"Well, I wouldn't start from here."

If you ever visit Ireland—and I believe you should—you'll quickly enjoy the Irish love of language. "Well, I wouldn't start from here" is poetic, philosophical, funny and true all at the same time.

When I hear most people's goals, I often feel I'm the man on the side of the road in Ireland. I'm often wondering, why did you start from here?

Art De Vany's great insight about fat loss, "Don't get fat in the first place," remains absolutely true… with a hint of cruelty. As we all know, the truth stings.

In terms of goal setting, it's far easier to prepare for law or medical school at age 12 when opportunity and momentum are on your side. Going to law school at night at age 30 while holding down a full-time job and keeping a family intact is far more difficult.

Notice this: I didn't say you can't get the goal. No. I don't like saying that. But… I wouldn't want to start from here.

That's the importance of elementary and high school education. It lines you up for a little bit easier route. Trying to undo the damage of drugs, alcohol and parties gets harder and harder as those years with "teen" in them come to a close.

It's better to try to lose 50 pounds now than to wait another year and have to lose 60. We all know this.

Like many truths, it's a sad truth.

Teach children the importance of goal setting early.

And if you're just coming around to a goal, good for you.

Start NOW! Don't wait until you're completely lost.

Show up

In 1996 in my administration newsletter, I wrote my three-point success formula:

1. Show up.

2. Don't quit.

3. Ask questions.

I'd like to think I invented it, but, like anything valuable in life, I had it handed down to me. This truth hit me in the face when I buried my brother, Phil. *The San Francisco Chronicle* published a lovely tribute to him and his volunteer work written by Lizzie Johnson.

She writes:

"How much of Phil's death can be attributed to the trauma of the fire, no one knows. But many people can't imagine Paradise without him.

"That's, in part, because Phil could be conned into anything— collecting cash at the ticket window before high school football games, dyeing his hair silver for his roles in the spring ballet, volunteering his time or his car or his movie collection. He did it, he said, because he loved his town. He would mutter and complain, so you knew it was a sacrifice, but he always showed up.

"If you committed to something, you followed through. Phil believed in that."

See the full article at:

https://www.sfchronicle.com/california-wildfires/article/He-tried-to-make-Paradise-all-its-name-14026656.php

I come from people who showed up. When their country called, they volunteered. When the neighbors down the street had a project, "we" had a project.

I swear half my victories come from the fact that I "showed up" and competed.

It's easy to say "Show up" or post or make a meme of it. In real life, though, it can be hard to do. Showing up means you get out of your comfy bed and spend a day pushing, pulling and hauling loads and loads of stuff up and down flights of stairs like my friends have done for me over and over. Chris Long and I used to joke we were Dumb and Dumber Moving Company long before there was a movie by that name.

You show up. Friends show up. Families show up.

And, if you're like my brother Phil, when you die, a thousand people show up to your Celebration of Life.

Because that's what good people do. They show up.

Planning the Plan

Years ago on a walk around some amazing archaeological sites in Ireland, the guide asked me if I had ever read the book *The Gnolls Credo*.

No, I had not... and what's a gnoll?

Josh Stanton's book introduces us to the half-hyena/half-human gnolls. The book is a fun read, but the real purpose of the book is to summarize the success philosophy of the gnolls. The guide summed the book with this brilliant, simple point:

> *Plan the Hunt.*
>
> *Hunt.*
>
> *Discuss the Hunt.*

The book fleshes this out in much more detail, but the point should be obvious for people seeking to start a new diet or training program.

Plan it.

Do it.

Now... talk about it. Now make it perfect.

That's the error most people make. The middle one is the tough one for most people... do it! We have all been to parties with nobody but experts in fitness, diet, politics, professional sports and all the world issues. Everybody has an opinion about everything. And we know about opinions. Everyone has one… and it doesn't stink.

There are a million plans for just about any and every approach you want to take for fitness, health, diet and longevity. They often contradict each other. It doesn't bother me that they do; in fact, I find insights in the friction of ideas rubbing against each other.

The key is to follow a plan. Two weeks or six weeks or whatever, follow the plan. Do it.

At a natural break, review it. Discuss it. Look for its limitations and issues. Truthfully, you might not find any!

It's okay to shift from an all-this diet to an all-that diet. In fact, your body… which seems to have a mad love affair with change… might revel in it. Sometimes changing the plan really works… after you followed the plan!

Listening to my inner Yoda, I can't help but think we need to "Do or don't do. There is no try."

Do!!!

People Tell You What They Think You Want to Hear

I've been working with humans since I can remember. We certainly are an interesting species. We can do amazing things, like travel to the deepest depths of the ocean and climb the tallest mountains.

Day to day, most of us don't lead the adventurer's life, cure diseases and hoist trophies. Sure, most of us have our moments, but we also have our bad days or weeks.

Or months. Or decades.

When working with clients in the area of goal setting, my ears seem to have a problem: People have extremely lofty goals! Yet, rarely, does anyone achieve them!

It took me years to understand this, and a quick discussion with the mirror helped me get my arms around this conundrum.

As I look back, I remember my mom asking me if I did my homework, my chores and my basic grooming and hygiene.

"Yes, yes, I did."

I had NOT done any of these things as I ran out to play. I told my mom what I thought she wanted to hear. Being the youngest of six, this never worked for me. She knew the real truth.

When you ask a fitness client, "What's your goal?" the answer is always perfect.

53

"I want to lose weight. I want to get back to daily exercise. I really want to be lean and trim again."

And… that's because this is what they think I want to hear. I ask a lot of questions when I assess people, and I strive to bring the person back to the "real." Reality is tough enough.

"Do you eat colorful vegetables every day?"

I had to add "colorful" because most people think potato and corn chips are veggies. The answer is usually, "Yes, yes, I do!"

"Do you exercise half an hour a day?

"Yes, yes, I do!"

Too bad. I can't help you because I was going to have you eat veggies and exercise half an hour a day. I'm sorry, I can't help you.

This tends to get people closer to the truth. This is where we get the long, drawn-out "Well…"

Finally, we get to the truth.

Usually, the truth is this: You see this person here? It's not me.

Our journey in fitness, health and longevity begins here: If I'm not me, how do I rediscover "me?"

With this insight, we begin the walk.

Fit

I'm not sure there is a more misunderstood word than "fit," especially when used in "fitness." But every jigsaw puzzle teaches us the true meaning: *Its pieces fit!*

The original term "fit" comes from the Old Nordic, "to knit." For me, that's the crucial point of why we eat a certain way, work out and sleep seriously.

A knitted person reflects the ideals of traditional western civilization: A person is body, mind, soul and spirit.

My buddy, Joe Courmier, taught me that life is like a tapestry. We combine all of these marvelous threads into something beautiful. All of us have an assortment of threads we're probably not proud to have in the final piece. Hopefully, we also have a collection of threads of wonderful, selfless acts that only a few people know about in this mortal life.

A good tapestry is well knitted. A good person is well knitted.

I've always considered a "fit" person to be one who can balance a working life with being a wonderful neighbor and family member… and still have time to eat properly and keep an appropriate bodyfat percentage.

If your kids hate you, your dog runs when you walk in the door, yet you maintain a six-pack ab wall, great for you. I'm not sure I can include you in my definition of "fit."

Fitness, Darwin taught us, is the ability to do a task. If the task is working on a desktop computer all day, well, you can certainly get by with less than glorious conditioning. But, when it comes time to carry a couch up several flights of stairs, the rules are going to change.

If you're racing swimmer, your measurement for fitness is a time. If you're a parent, we'll look at some other things. "Fit" changes from situation to situation.

Be the person your friends call in emergencies… or to move a couch up a flight of stairs.

Fit in, stay fit, fit into your clothes, be fighting fit, fit as a fiddle, fit like a glove, fit and trim, fit the bill and be fit as a king.

Be fit to do the tasks of life for as long as you can. Be knitted.

Never Fail. Unless You Do.

I don't like sharing this story. It's got some funny things in it, but I don't like it.

Well, let's get to it.

We had a pretty good-sized group of throwers in Arlington, Texas. My brother, Gary, competed too, and we had a host of people cheer us along in the National Weight Pentathlon Championships.

My training had me on track to not only break the American record, but I was fairly sure the world record would go down too. I'd been bringing up my weaker events—the javelin and hammer *(it's five events: hammer, discus, shot put, javelin and 35-pound weight throw)*—and my Highland Game success had given me a lot of experience in competing for hours in the hot sun.

With the first event, the hammer, behind me, I was way ahead of what I'd planned. Going into the discus, by far my best event, I started counting my chickens. And here's the thing: I JUST KNEW I was going to do better and better in every event.

There's a thing we call "on."

I was on.

My warmups in the discus, easy efforts, were just flat-out "wow."

As I entered the ring for my first throw, I felt very good.

I got to the back of the ring, breathed out, smiled and began my wind up, and…

"Where did you get that sandwich?"

"All the officials get lunch."

"Is that a cheese sandwich?"

"Yeah, I got a cheese sandwich."

My wife noticed something. I stepped back and shook out my head. By GOD! A cheese sandwich conversation. The two ring judges were speaking to each other across the cages, and I was in the middle.

Folks, I've had competitors call me out for my school and my race. I've had a guy call my wife a bitch during a game. He paid a VERY high price on the next play. I've competed in snowstorms, Pacific storms, lightning delays, darkness and probably everything else nature can throw at a thrower.

I've never had to deal with a cheese sandwich. Or, better stated, a lack of a cheese sandwich.

They kept talking. They got in my head. The discus throw was a disaster for me that day, and I barely got a single legal mark.

The only highlight was when the meet director told me—I'm sure he meant it nicely—that I was the first person to ever lose with a score of over 4,000 points. I took second to a hammer specialist.

Cheers to me.

I hate this story. It taught me some good lessons I've expanded into a whole program (see my book, *Now What?* for details), but the key lesson was this:

People can be ignorant.

Ignorant is NOT stupid. Ignorance is the quality of IGNORING things, like being quiet when a person is performing.

Not long after, there was a seniors meet at BYU. Now, I still don't know why some meets are for seniors and others meets are for masters, but I'm just a discus thrower.

I don't like BYU. Sorry. And everybody knows that. Maybe it's because I say it a lot.

The ring judge at this meet also thought he was a combination of comedian and social commentator. When someone entered the ring, he'd attempt to be funny. With me, as I entered on my first throw, he made a "joke" I'm sure he thought was funny:

"Just pretend Hillary Clinton's face is in the middle of the sector."

I'm sure he assumed that, as a white middle-aged man in Utah, I shared his political beliefs and his misogynist vision of the world.

I don't.

A friend of mine noted that I stopped, looked at him in a way that shut him up, and threw my discus.

Far.

I had taught myself to ignore ignorance.

Failure is a wonderful instructor. Failure teaches me so much more clearly than success. I just hate failure so much.

I also hate cheese sandwiches.

Life Lessons—Some Tough, All True

Resumé Building versus Eulogy Building

I recently had one of those odd things happen: I got an email asking for my resumé/vita. It was the same day I was preparing to speak at my brother's funeral.

There's nothing new here. Other brighter minds have discussed this before me, but I couldn't ignore the reality. In life, we have two kinds of documents:

Resumés

Eulogies

The resumé is that wonderful few pieces of paper that tells the world you're able to take on the task of junior senior manager of small things at the wingernut factory. You got the degree; you sat in the chair; you paid your dues and, for the most part, avoided imprisonment.

Good for you! You never got caught!

"Eulogy" literally means "the good story." In a eulogy, people might miss the degrees from the universities, the committees and the councils. What they'll talk about is when you showed up, helped out and made a difference.

At my brother's funeral, one of my cousins said, "I need to volunteer more." Five words. In those five words, Jane told me the impact of Phil's funeral upon her.

I need to volunteer more.

Showing up and making a difference doesn't go on the resumé.

It goes in the eulogy.

A resumé is nice for slapping down on a desk and telling a person you're worthy of a position.

The eulogy tells the world why you should never be forgotten.

Certainly, focus on both. But, know which is more important.

Eat the Biggest, Ugliest Toad First

My wife, Tiffini, federal agent and philosopher, often reminds me of this:

"If you have to eat a plate of toads, find the biggest, ugliest one. Eat that one first. Then, all the other toads won't seem so bad."

For the record, we don't eat toads in our home.

Yet.

The point of this, of course, is if you have a series of nasty tasks, pick the worst first. I used this as an administrator, and once had a woman at a meeting tell me she knew she was in trouble if I called at 8:45 in the morning.

I got to my office at 8:30. I turned everything on, answered voicemail (back when people answered voicemail), opened my to-do list and circled the biggest, ugliest toad. I started my day knocking off ugly toads.

At 9:00am, I had pleasant sailing the rest of the day as all the nasty, ugly, brutish stuff was behind me. I'd then take care of my monthly checklist, and spend the rest of the day doing what I consider the key to administration: wandering around.

I'd go on the road to meet people in their offices to see the problems from their perspective. I'd drop by the printers to see how we could do things better next time. I managed by knowing the people and the problems from their vantage points.

In my lofty office, I was nearly always wrong about what I thought was the problem in the field. In the field, there were other toads jumping up and down and leaptoading from here to there and messing up the flow of things.

When I got back to the office the next day, I'd grab my phone and deal with the biggest, ugliest toads.

When it comes to training, do the thing you hate to do first. Usually, for most people, it's leg work, like front squats. When it comes to financial planning, usually it's an honest look at debt.

Find the big toads.

And... eat them.

It's Not What You Eat, It's What You Ate

It's a rare day when I don't hear something about diet, food or nutrition. There's a magic supplement "they" talked about on television. There's evidence that low this or high that "burns fat." And, of course, the person telling me this is going to start doing this diet or magic formula to shed those unwanted pounds.

"Gonna."

It's a word my mother hated. "I'm going gonna do this." "I'm gonna do that." Although she may not have been a recognized philosopher, her insight was profound: It's not what you're gonna do, it's what you're doing.

And, sadly for some, it's what you did.

I recently heard that you're literally the sum of all of your life choices. Some days, I might hear that idea and think, "You know, I did good."

And, of course, as I think deeper, at times I wish I would have had the knight in *Indiana Jones* standing close to tell me, "Choose wisely." Occasionally, I choose poorly. I've made my share of dumb decisions.

In the world of personal training, most clients show up asking for one thing: to lose weight. Now, and I can't beat this to death enough, losing weight is easy. Let me cut off one of your legs.

Done!

Losing fat is what people want. As I've already noted, the easiest route to losing fat, to quote Art De Vany, is: "Don't get fat in the first place."

When he said this, the questioner wanted to kill him.

This is the truest truth: It's not what you're going to eat, it's what you ate.

Parents, train your children to eat home-cooked food filled with quality ingredients loaded with vegetables, appropriate protein and love. Have them eat in community without distractions as often as you can. Let them learn to enrich food with herbs and spices, not deep frying and sugar. When they go off to college, don't pick up the tab for nightly binges of pizza and beer. Fight the dreaded freshman 15/40 with all your might.

And if, as many people have told me happened to them, one day you "wake up fat," you're going to battle this in the kitchen. Fat loss happens in the kitchen. You may have to fast, you may have to eat loads of veggies, and you may have to begin a strength training program.

It's what we're gonna do.

Practice Thanksgiving

I love celebrations and parties and everything that goes with them. I put up Christmas decorations early, and love the various pageants and parades that go with holidays. We take the family up to the Yuletide train ride every year, with hot chocolate, and we look for every opportunity to find fun.

With the pressures of the holidays, we learned an important lesson years ago: We don't have to celebrate on the designated day. We have married family members whose holidays consist of gathering at this grandma's house, the other one there, then off to someone else's and on and on. The same caravan drives from place to place to place, always late and running behind.

What joy.

The stress of typing that bothered me. We excused ourselves from the major holidays years ago. We love Thanksgiving and the wonderful LACK of a lot of stresses that go with other events. Multiple times a year, we call in family and friends to a "Practice Thanksgiving." It can be any day or time of year, and we roast our turkey and put out plenty of veggies and good cheer.

If we forget something, it's fine. It's just practice.

If you can't make it, no one minds because, as we all know, it's just practice.

We're especially thankful no one has to pick up and leave to go somewhere else.

It's seems, I've discovered with dismay, that no one else practices Practice Thanksgiving. Madness!

With the married couples in the family, our Christmas traditions were quickly muddled with other traditions of the in-laws.

And that's GOOD! But it's also hard to schedule.

So, we invented a Christmas holiday of our own:

Christmas Adam.

It's the day before Christmas Eve. Get it? Adam before Eve?

The upside? Nobody has anything scheduled that night. It's an open night, and no one has this tradition. No conflicts with schedules leads to no conflicts with the party participants.

I look for every reason I can to celebrate. Life can be miserable at times… we all experience those rough patches of life. Yet no matter how things turn, the thought of a happy gathering keeps me going.

I don't wait for the traditional holidays—along with the traditional holiday clutter—to bring my loved ones together.

We invent gatherings as often as we can. It's good practice.

Mindful or Mindless Habits

I've spent my life training people in the weightroom and field of play. At the same time, I've stood at the podium and lectured on theology, religious studies and religious education. Coaching and religion seem to find common ground in many answers, but one in particular: free will.

Almost everyone thinks that they, if they wanted to, can suddenly flick on the switch of absolute focused self-discipline. In a moment, if you listen closely at a party, many people can turn their lives around in a complete 180. Or, as my assistant coach used to say, "We need to do a complete 360."

I'm not sure he understood where this would put him.

Certainly in the historic record, we find stories of individuals who have done this feat of will. I just don't see it very often. In many cases, we hear that someone had to hit rock bottom in order to climb out. Maybe given the option of death or exercise, there are some who popped up and started moving. But, for most of us, changing direction in life is NOT like flicking a light switch.

As much as I believe in free will—the ability to choose, even if it's just what one thinks about a situation—I don't think many people can summon it enough to turn this 180. Listen: I know I can't. That's why I rely on two things for everything I do:

Habits

Community

71

Coach Ralph Maughan told me in 1977 to "make myself a slave to good habits." I probably take this too far, but I know this: Everything we do mindlessly is a habit.

I simply try to make my mindless things good.

Shopping lists and menus will do more for your health than those products they sell on TV that guarantee fat loss or whatever. Having a basic wardrobe of things that work together will save time every day. I keep floss sticks in my car and floss on the way to the gym. It's mindless, but my dental hygienist compliments me every time.

If it's true we're the sum of our five dearest friends, it might be worth your time to seek out extremely kind, successful and fit buddies to pal around with. To work out, I invite people from literally everywhere to train with me. Humans are communal animals, and we seem to do best in community.

I offer a place to train, experience and coaching. The community shows up to my house and it gets me out the door to train! It's not my free will getting me to do my conditioning; it's people knocking on my door.

If you want to make your complete 180, rethink your morning and evening rituals—your most important habits—and invite the world to help you with your goals. It works.

Pecked to Death by Ducks

Tiffini has a funny way of explaining parenthood: "It's like being pecked to death by ducks." Kelly, my daughter, certainly doesn't like this, but her ringtone is "Quack, quack... quack, quack."

Mornings with school kids are something that have to be experienced. No matter how well I prepared, it didn't matter. Breakfast in the slow cooker from the night before, clothes laid out (uniforms in our case, God bless them!), backpacks set up and the day sorted out... well, it simply didn't matter.

Every day, there was something: science report, unread book, or "we need $12 in nickels for a project."

By the time we dropped the kids off at school, my mind was fried and my nerves were frazzled. Every day, I'd strive to make the morning better, and every day, the ducks would find a new place to peck.

We did well, honestly. Menus, chore lists, weekly checklists, monthly checklists and shopping lists kept things less crazy. I can't honestly say it was NOT crazy, but day by day, month by month and year by year, things worked out very well.

You have to look at your life sometimes and ask a big question: "What are my ducks?"

What are those nagging things that eat up most of our brain space? It's not just kids. It could be debt, health, loss, fear or any of a million issues.

My advice? First, take a moment to recognize what's pecking you. If it's debt, get out a pen and paper, write out your debts and review the hole you're in. Look at that number. Then, think.

Thinking is underrated… I think.

One thing that helped us years ago was to find the debt with the lowest number. Pay it off. Then, as you can, pay off the next lowest. If you can unburden something, let it go… sell it. Hell, give it away. Spending time, money and emotional energy on a car in the driveway that "one day" you'll restore is a big old pecking duck.

You neighbors will like it gone, too.

Ducks.

Name them. Label them. Say it out loud.

Think a little about how you can… dare I say… get your ducks in a row.

Cycles

Everything works. That's a fundamental principle of training I discovered over and over in my career.

Well, everything works for about six weeks. My friend, Dan Martin, calls me "Mister 43" because after about six weeks (42 days), every wonderful program, plan, diet and idea seems to come to a crushing halt.

Here's the thing: The smart people figure this out.

Marty Gallagher decided years ago that the standard bodybuilding diet of six meals a day is right. But, the concept of one meal a day, the Warrior Diet that was popular at the turn of the millennium is true too. Why not do both? Marty suggests a few months on one, then shift to the other. Enjoy.

Oddly, the body seems to love fasting. And it tends to love feasting. Religions remind us that the "fast comes before the feast," but changing things up always seems to work.

Lyle McDonald, one of the greatest minds in nutrition, taught me this years ago with his Cyclical Ketogenic Diet. I followed this for a while, and made some of my elite throwers practice it. CKD is about five days of no or low carb followed by a two-day carb up.

Throwers did really well competing without carbs in the system. It made them cranky, irritable and ready to kill. Oddly, that's a perfect mindset for the shot put, hammer, discus and Highland Games. After the contest, a few pizzas and beer would make them fall in love with life, and just want to hug.

Not a good mindset for throwing!

Recently, I've fallen in love with the monthly fast originated by Valter Longo, the Fast Mimicking Diet. For a few days, I eat nuts, olives and veggies. I keep my calories low and allow my body to scramble to rebuild itself (autophagy) with only 800 calories and virtually no protein. After a few days, my tummy is clearly smaller, my skin looks great and my pants get loose. It's only three to five days, but the results... oddly... stay. And, often, the results improve!

Certainly, there is magic in FMD. But it could simply be that the body loves changing. I began my writing career by recommending we train according to seasons. In a nutshell (along with some olives), here you go:

- Winter: Go heavy, Go hard, Go home.

- Spring: Get outside as you can, play and enjoy the air.

- Summer: Swim, bike, run, play. Enjoy the sun!

- Fall: Back to school time. This is when you do those regimented training programs.

In other words, sometimes you train hard in the gym and sometimes you play. With food, sometimes you should eat a lot of veggies, and sometimes you should shovel down more protein. Change things up occasionally. With your diet and exercise program, enjoy a bit of everything.

Your health and fitness will thank you for it.

Level Training

I'm not sure I have a humble opinion about anything, but I think the biggest gaps in training are instantly apparent in real-world application. There's something lacking in so many programs, but once you see it, like those illusions that just pop out at you when you finally see the trophy or dog or whatever, it becomes hard to not see it.

Generally, the two biggest gaps are authentic squatting (not accordion squatting) and any and all loaded carries. In real life, like extended hiking trips, both of these gaps will become obvious on the first potty break. If you haven't been doing loaded carries, you will pay a high price ascending the Himalayas… or helping your friends move.

Adding goblet squats and farmer walks has been a game-changing addition for many of the people and programs I work with professionally.

So, do them.

Yet, people often miss another more subtle issue: the lack of levels. I'm not calling out Curves or Nautilus, but an entire workout basically sitting down in chairs while seatbelted doesn't reflect the demands of most of life.

Sitting down is one level. "Level" is the word I use to describe the ground, half kneeling, full kneeling, lunge position, fully erect and moving away in various directions. Think of the levels in the earth's crust—as a geography minor in college, I occasionally like to flex my knowledge of the planet.

Some movements, like the Turkish getup, involve all the steps up and down. Combining a waiter's walk into the top position moves us in virtually all of our levels. And, as good as TGUs are, these are just not dynamic enough for every purpose.

That's why I like combining movements in a training session. We've been using lift-n-sprints for decades (I used to call them Litvinovs, but got tired of defending the name), and the results on the field of play have been amazing.

Pick a hinge or squat variation, do about 10, drop the load and INSTANTLY sprint away. Vary the load and distance, but not the intensity. There is only one coaching cue:

Go, go, go!!!

Hooking up a sled also works if you're smart enough to not put the load in the path of the sled. It's funny to watch when people don't listen to the warning of keeping the load from the sled's path. We'll call these lift-n-sleds.

As great as these are, many of us train in smaller spaces. This combination works wonders for the body:

> *Eight goblet squats*
>
> *Prowler push... as appropriate, but 20–40 meters is great*
>
> *Eight pushups*

You will feel the hit from getting up and down off the ground and the changes in levels. Up to five rounds of this workout is appropriate, but strive for less at first.

My best is 20 loops: 160 goblet squats, 160 pushups and 400 meters of the prowler. I was tired.

If you don't have the space to prowl, sled or sprint, the swing + goblet squat + pushup combination works well here. I've noted this before, but a review may help.

My favorite is the humane burpee. Dan Martin gave us this name and I can't think of a better term. You can certainly make this harder or easier, but just do the basic example first.

Be sure to follow the advice about reps on the goblet squat and pushup. We want the reps to descend as we move through the humane burpee, hence the name "humane."

So, here you go:

> *15 Swings*
> *5 Goblet squats*
> *5 Pushups*
> *15 Swings*
> *4 Goblet squats*
> *4 Pushups*
> *15 Swings*
> *3 Goblet squats*
> *3 Pushups*
> *15 Swings*
> *2 Goblet squats*
> *2 Pushups*
> *15 Swings*
> *1 Goblet squat*
> *1 Pushup*

That comes out to 75 swings, 15 goblet squats and 15 pushups. The real exercise seems to be the popping up and down for the pushups. Most of us don't take any rest through the workout, but feel free to stop if you need to rest.

Mixing barbell deadlifts with bear crawls is a wonderful preseason prep workout for American football.

Once you begin to embrace training the levels, you'll find your eyes will quickly pick up the total lack of this kind of training done by most people. It raises the heart rate, adds work capacity and reflects the real world of sport and life.

Get leveled.

DIEting from a Foods Approach

I use a simple 1–2–3–4 assessment with "normal" people. Athletes are a bit different to assess: I simply ask, "Can you go?" The book with the assessment is called, not shockingly, *Can You Go?*

And that's it!

The assessment with the general population is:

- *One:* Stand on one foot.

- *Two:* Two measurements (over or under 300 pounds and waistline measurement).

- *Three:* I ask three questions.

- *Four:* We do four simple tests, although the first one (a plank) gives us the bulk of the information.

The second question of the three is fairly simple:

Do you eat colorful veggies?

And, of course, everyone answers "yes." We like to lie to ourselves. This question opens a door to a fascinating discussion. Often, many adults CAN'T eat veggies because of dental issues, so, you know:

Go to the dentist! Floss your teeth (tooth… whatever).

It's true. I go to the dentist three times a year because that's recommended. I floss twice a day, because… that's what we should do. I can eat veggies because I have my healthy teeth. I have other ways to ask this question:

Do you eat like an adult?

Do you eat "clean?"

Do you have a menu and shopping list?

Do you practice fasting?

In *Mass Made Simple*, I wrote this:

"Here is an idea: Eat like an adult. Stop eating fast food, stop eating kid's cereal, knock it off with all the sweets and comfort foods whenever your favorite show is not on when you want it on, ease up on the snacking and—don't act like you don't know this— eat vegetables and fruits more. Really, how difficult is this? Stop with the whining. Stop with the excuses. Act like an adult and stop eating like a television commercial. Grow up."

It became one of my most-quoted bits and, at some level, it seems to resonate with people. Some people hate the paragraph, but they understand it.

Truly, if a person has a menu and a shopping list and prepares meals as regularly as looking at TV or the internet, we wouldn't have much to discuss in the field of fitness and nutrition.

In 1984, the nutritionist at the Olympic training center told us: *"I don't see what the big deal is. Eat protein and veggies. Drink water."*

Years later, Robb Wolf told me the secret to performance dieting:

More fiber

More protein

More fish oil

Again, it's all pretty simple.

> *"Really, how difficult is this? Stop with the whining. Stop with the excuses. Act like an adult and stop eating like a television commercial. Grow up."*

Sorry. That seems to pop out of my mind occasionally.

I can see the hands coming up. "Dan, I'm allergic to X, Y and Z."

Don't eat them.

But, look at this list from the American Lung Association:

MOST ALLERGENIC FOODS

Peanuts

Fish

Egg

Milk

Wheat

Soy

Fish and eggs surprised me, but the rest of them are, as we read this today, probably as far from nature as a plastic straw.

Many people struggle with milk and wheat—in college, we were told 95% of the population had issues with one or both. Milk is famously inconsumable for many groups.

In contrast, Dr. Elson Haas, in an interview with *Mind and Muscle Power,* gave us this list of the most tolerable foods:

MOST TOLERABLE FOODS

Rice

Pears

Lamb

Kale

Salmon (and other deep-sea fish, like halibut and sole)

Trout

Turkey

Rabbit

Sweet potatoes

Honey

He goes on to recommend cabbage, carrots, cauliflower, broccoli, apricots, beets, squashes, olives, olive oil, cranberries, herbal teas and tapioca.

I quickly began to see a pattern here. Humans seem to feel better with foods not tampered much.

The least allergenic food list and Haas's recommendations seem to tie in well with Brad Pilon's work in *Good Belly Bad Belly*. This is the list of foods that have the best micronutrient profile:

BEST POLYPHENOL FOODS

Dark chocolate

Blueberries

Olives (green and black)

Black currants

Plums

Cherries

Blackberries

Cloves

Hazelnuts

Pecans

Orange juice

Red wine

Dark coffee

That's not a terrible list of foods. You don't often hear, "I'm going make you eat chocolate and drink wine until you come around in conditioning!"

I like to quote an old *Men's Journal* article on magic foods. This was the list I used to compile my "perfect diet." My Perfect Diet (patent pending) allows you to eat ANYTHING you want AFTER you eat two pounds of salmon, a dozen eggs, three handfuls of almonds, a pound of beef and two large servings of real yogurt each day. After that, eat anything you like. Good luck on that.

THE SUPER FOODS

Eggs

Almonds

Salmon

Yogurt

Beef

Olive oil

Water

Coffee

As you review the lists, you might find that certain things "win."

FOR THE WIN

Coffee

Water

> *Salmon*
>
> *The olive family*

Let's sum this simply:

> *Eat closer to nature.*
>
> *Eat protein and veggies.*
>
> *Drink water (and coffee... and wine!).*

And... you KNOW this!!!!

Some Big Ideas about Training ... and Life

Fluid and Crystallized Intelligence

In the 1940s, Raymond Catell came up with an amazing insight into how people think. He summarized intelligence into two kinds: fluid intelligence and crystallized intelligence.

Fluid intelligence is the skill to reason, analyze, and solve unforeseen problems. Whether this is right or not, some people would say this is the big engine of intelligence. Innovators seem to have this in abundance. I often use this quote from Warren Buffet to explain this:

> *"First come the innovators, who see opportunities that others don't and champion new ideas that create genuine value. Then come the imitators, who copy what the innovators have done. Sometimes they improve on the original idea; often they tarnish it. Last come the idiots, whose avarice undermines the very innovations they are trying to exploit."*

Crystallized intelligence is the skill to use the accumulated knowledge of humankind. Some of us are libraries of knowledge (and wisdom), and easily know how to use these volumes. Crystallized intelligence tends to expand through life from both personal and community experiences. When we all lean in when grandpa talks, we're gathering crystallized intelligence.

Fluid and crystallized intelligence are important resources for walking through life.

Let me add one more thing: warrior and king (queen) thinking.

While attaining my first master's degree, I did a deep dive into *Beowulf*, the epic poem, under the guidance of two professors, Norm Jones and Robert Cole. I went through every line looking for patterns; finally, one leaped out to me.

Speeches.

When warriors speak, they only speak in the pure present. The past doesn't matter and there may not be a future. Athletes, young children and artists tend to do this. Athletes and artists are often judged simply on that last performance.

Kings and queens tend to speak differently. They discuss the past, what brought us here to the present and ideally, how what we do here will impact the future. Lincoln's *Gettysburg Address* is the perfect example of this concept.

Let's combine these concepts into a quadrant and discuss them.

	WARRIOR THINKING	**KING THINKING**
FLUID INTELLIGENCE	Reaction to something new	Good coaching
CRYSTALLIZED INTELLIGENCE	Yoda and the martial arts	Mentoring

FLUID INTELLIGENCE AND WARRIOR THINKING

We were joking the other day that no one ever got butt dialed with a rotary phone. If you could go back in time—probably never a good idea—explaining butt dialing to your great-grandparents would be something worthy of sharing on social media... I mean video... wait, I mean, 8mm film.

Wait… cave paintings?

Parents today have concerns that might not have been faced by any other generation. Your teen daughter striking up a friendship with "my new bestest friend online, and I want to go to Europe to meet her" is something no one ever said until now.

No, I wouldn't let her go. I'd alert the authorities.

When faced with novel problems, we still need to find answers.

In sports, things change radically with the advent of GPS measurements, computers and video on the sidelines and massive databases with every possible output. Computer guys have radically changed professional baseball and basketball by showing the teams that conventional wisdom is often wrong in the face of facts.

In American football, there is a certain madness in the modern offense that doesn't huddle, doesn't pause, and throws the ball everywhere and anywhere on every play. The coaching staff can't take a timeout for every new trick formation, nor can they prepare for literally everything.

This is the time for athletes, playing in the "now," the pure present, with the need to make rapid, fluid decisions and… in the time it took for me to type this, the play started and the athletes made the play. It's that fast.

Certainly, it helps to have principles. For example, Bear Bryant used to try to keep his defenders working like spokes on a bicycle—everyone is connected to a central hub. This can be taught by "rules" as simple as, "One can hurt me, two can kill me," or "He goes/I stay," or whatever summarizes 50 pages of a playbook in one quick phrase.

But something new always shows up. Something different. Something strange. Something that breaks the rules.

Adapt. Decide. Go.

That's fluid intelligence and warrior thinking… adapt, decide, go.

Crystallized Intelligence and Warrior Thinking

In 1977, I sat in Gregor Winslow's Audi Fox as we pulled up to the speaker at the drive-in theater. We then pulled out the lawn chairs, and got ready for a new film to begin:

Star Wars

Now, this is the original and, along with *The Empire Strikes Back*, changed not only movie watching—along with *Jaws,* these became the summer blockbusters—but it changed the conversation for many people. Suddenly, people were talking a bit differently:

"That's why you fail."

"Adventure. Excitement. A Jedi craves not these things."

"Do. Or do not. There is no try."

You might recognize the words of Master Yoda here. The Jedi knights, as well as most martial arts traditions, have generations of traditions that help shape the vision of the modern practitioner.

Much like religions—religion comes from the root "link back"— these traditions link back to their founder's vision, and keep the current generations true to these foundations.

This knowledge is brick and mortar: crystallized knowledge.

But the actions must be in the now... no thinking, no judging, just action. Both Yoda and the martial arts masters would agree that we do. Or we do not. There is no try.

True mastery is so simple, so elegant that we might miss what we see.

There's a wonderful story by Ryszard Kapuscinski about watching the discus throwing great Edmund Piatowski during a practice session. Ryszard sits down next to a local man, and Kapuscinski notes the man is wearing a sweater. The local tells him he has heard that today Edmund might break the world record. Piatowski throws and throws.

Finally, his coach announces to all gathered that, indeed, one traveled over the world record. The local laments that he expected to see something more... perhaps exciting.

When the foundations are set firmly and the effort is effortless, the audience often misses the excellence.

It's too simple. It's too smooth.

But the performance is lovely. We expect more and the "more" comes from less.

But the audience wants excitement.

Excitement. A Jedi craves not these things.

Fluid Intelligence and King or Queen Thinking

Change is hard.

Especially as we age, change is hard.

Yet, change also brings safety, health, wonder and comfort. Clean drinking water, by itself, might be responsible for you being able to read this little essay. Doctors fought against washing their hands before surgery… even after autopsies… for a long time. They didn't want change.

If you want to get into the wisdom business—that lucrative field where you give advice that no one takes but later wishes they did—you need to be able to embrace change appropriately.

Years ago, a young man named Dick Fosbury came up with a different method of high jumping. He battled his coaches daily to allow him to jump his way. The track and field world found him to be more of a circus sideshow than an actual athlete. His gold medal at the Olympics changed a few minds, but most still fought against his method.

Today, literally every high jumper in the world embraces his technique. In an event that strains the human body against the most basic of Newton's laws and gravity, this technique has destroyed old marks that used other methods.

My college coach was a master of fluid intelligence and kingly vision. When one of his athletes came to him and told him he'd added 20 feet to his best discus throw by having a "wide leg," Coach took him to the ring and had him demonstrate.

In minutes, Coach Maughan rethought and refocused his coaching with this idea. In track and field, we constantly face the challenge of faster and farther. It's been true since Ulysses won the discus throw in *The Odyssey*. Our "novel" problem, faster and farther, is a permanent challenge.

Coach had the skill to see that what happened in the past was good, but THIS is better. And, years later, he taught me this refinement.

Change is hard. Change is often better.

Unless it's not.

By keeping an eye on the lessons of the past, wisdom allows us to see how this new development may help us down the line. That's thinking like a king or queen.

Crystallized Intelligence and King or Queen Thinking

Back in the 1980s, PBS offered us a show, *The Power of Myth*, with Bill Moyers interviewing Joseph Campbell. Moyers would ask a question and Campbell would sweep off into a dozen legends, myths and stories connecting the inner world with the self and the universe.

It became "must-see TV" before the creation of the phrase.

For most of human history, we had these wonderful people who could sit near the fire and tell the tales of what it means to be "us." These storytellers reached deep into our collective history and extolled the virtues and values of our shared community and reminded us of who we are.

My mother's most damaging condemnation of me happened after a football game when I picked up several personal foul penalties. She simply told me, "That's not who we are."

Telemachus's teacher, Mentor, was so truthful and truth seeking (with the help of the gods) that his name continues down to us as the wise elder who keeps us on the path. T. H. White's Merlyn instructs young Arthur in the ways of the world through both experience and wise counsel.

We need both: experience and wise council.

We must be allowed to make mistakes and enjoy success.

We need those brick and mortar experiences from breaking a limb climbing a tree to working together as a team to cement our adult lives.

Our stories soon mix with the storyteller's adventures and we become what our community hoped for—a reasonable member able to help when needed and help when it's simply the right thing to do.

Our legacies are the foundations of a future we will probably never see. Perhaps we shouldn't see it; it's up to the future storytellers to tell our stories without our meddling.

The need for this depth of our collective wisdom is instinctive. It's part of what makes us human—it's the glue that defines humanity.

Improving Skills ... or Not

I love sports. I love watching people (and sometimes dogs, horses and boats) make instant decisions that make or break years of preparation. I often ask coaches and players a simple question:

"What are the three things that impact victory... make you win?

I had a famous basketball coach answer this in an instant:

1. Free throws when tired

2. Offensive rebounds

3. Transition defense

He nodded gravely, even though I had no clue about that third one. A fighter pilot once answered this with:

1. Speed is life

2. Hit and run

3. Straight lines... no hooks

He went on to describe these as all basically the same, but failure to adhere to these lessons was a "bad choice."

These are all things that win.

We also have a bunch of necessary stuff. Obviously, for the basketball coach, there were lots of things like ball handling, situational plays, layups and a host of other skills and equipment demands. Uniforms are nice to have.

This leads us to an important point: There are skills that CAN be improved and some that CAN'T. Wish all you like for really tall kids, over seven feet, and tell me how that goes.

In some sports, like baseball, a similar skill like catching a ball can be improved, like catching high fly balls, and some seem to be difficult to improve, like catching a screaming ground ball right off the batter's bat.

Genetics and geography can't be improved. A fast-twitch kid from Canada will play hockey; the same kid might wrestle in Iowa and Olympic lift in Bulgaria. Surfers tend to come from California and Hawaii, and you don't find a lot of elite rodeo riders from New York City.

The Key to Coaching (and Life)
Things that Win and Skills that Can Be Improved

I always tell people that what you do in the first 10 minutes of training tells me everything I need to know about what you're doing. If you pop into the gym and begin with front squats or Olympic lifts, I get the sense you're fairly serious about training. If you begin foam rolling on the ground while reading your phone, I make another judgment.

In every sport, and everything in life, there are winning elements. Raising good kids has little to do with money, but a lot to do with quality time. If you wish to have that same wasp waistline deep into life, less time eating fast food and more time eating quality food is probably "winning."

If winning is "free throws when tired," practicing this skill will probably help your chances of winning. That's obvious. Focusing on this truth separates the greats from the less-great. If you're a discus thrower and only do standing throws, you're NOT doing those things that win and can be improved.

Every team usually has a list of things on the wall that highlight things that win. "No turnovers." "Commit to excellence." I've always been a fan of the only sign at the New England Patriot's locker room: Do your job.

Generally, we know what wins. The key is to find the skills that can be improved that lead to victory.

These are the twin towers of successful coaching: discovering those winning parts and the skills that can be improved. Focusing on this list will win more games and championships over time than focusing on the other stuff.

The problem, of course, is finding those items. In track and field, practicing the event along with basic strength training might be all one needs to do.

To figure out what these keys are, I recommend *The Prisoner's Dilemma*. The idea is, for whatever reason, you're only allowed three 15-minute sessions a week to practice your sport or goal. With these time constrictions, you won't warm up or do yoga, you will… what?

Your answer is probably the elements that win and skills that can be improved.

I asked Josh Hillis this question about fat loss and he answered: "Food prep!" Josh reminds us that food prep is what wins in fat loss and it can be improved.

Things that Are Needed and Skills that Can't Be Improved

I had a talk with John Colosimo a few years ago. He was lamenting how it was easier being a track coach (like me) than an American football coach (like him). As always, the grass is greener and easier to mow on the other side of the astroturf. He noted that I could have a season without any sprinters, but he had to have a left tackle… no matter how awful the player was on the field.

In American football, the offense, by rule, needs seven men on the line of scrimmage. You "need" this. You also need a field, officials, a ball and thousands of other things too. But, as all good coaches know, you can hide the players who can't play very well.

There are plants you can buy at the store that need water and adequate sunlight. Raising plants is pretty easy. Now, go to the shelter and find a puppy (ideally a hunting dog because they love families), and figure out what the puppy needs. Then, bring home a baby and the list goes vertical fast!

The things you need are very important to success. YES, you need to host a full team, but often what wins is something else.

There are skills that can't be improved. The sign of a good coach, teacher or mentor is the ability to appreciate that some things, most obviously height and speed (and brains, as we all discover), simply don't get better. In baseball, bunting gets better with practice, but rarely do pitchers throw much faster even with the best coaching.

Most coaches realize that playing hard, playing defense, being aggressive and hustling are all skills we can improve.

So, improve them.

Other skills… well, with some skills you have to take what you get. Focus on what you CAN improve, and not what you WISH you could improve.

	THINGS THAT WIN	THINGS THAT ARE NEEDED
SKILLS THAT CAN BE IMPROVED		
SKILLS THAT CAN'T BE IMPROVED		

As you prepare for anything in the world of sports—and life— think through this little chart. You have to do what's needed. You might get lucky and find some needs that can be improved.

Finding the things that win that can be improved is, obviously, the key to success.

Training for the Crazy Life

It's going to be your turn one day.

We don't appreciate how we tend to sleep walk through much of life until, well, "it's your turn."

In college and high school, we roll out of bed, toss down some cereal and move patiently from room to room, learning from someone else. Then, off to activities, athletics or whatever. Maybe Mom or Dad makes you dinner, and it's time for relaxing after this hectic day of truly just showing up.

Soon, though, it's your turn. Your older child freaks at breakfast because the report assigned weeks ago is due today, and she needs a diorama of the Battle of Midway. The younger one decides to hate everything, the dropoff line at school is backed up, the boss is expecting the Willewagon report to be resubmitted and traffic is bad to awful. When you pick up the kids from school, it's your fault… for everything.

It's at these times, you ask someone to help you get back into shape. In many cases, the "shape" is round, and getting back into any other shape is going to be difficult. After getting brilliant and ill-fitting advice from the internet, you sign up for the most recent crazy, confusing fad you can find.

Usually, it involves someone screaming about the "burn."

Hey, your life is burning around you. You don't need more burn.

If your life is crazy, you need sanity in your training. Waking up a half hour earlier will not only reset your hormones—one researcher argues that proper hormones comes down to two things: going to bed within two hours of sundown and moving the moment you awaken—but it might give you that alone time you crave. If you bring the love of your life, this walk will do wonders for furthering the relationship.

Certainly, train. Somehow. I had a home gym during the craziest periods of my life, and I often got my workout done while prepping meals or doing the laundry.

Fold towels, then front squat—I should sell this program!

I did goblet squats, simple carries, pushups and pullups. Nothing fancy here, folks.

Here's what you can do during the crazy life: The basics. The foundational work. The simple stuff.

Don't try to pack on a crazy life with crazy training.

It's the path to the crazy train.

Coaching Basics

I was asked a simple question: What ideas about strength and conditioning do you have that are unconventional?

My answer: None.

The person asking the question was shocked. With the follow-up, he asked about some of the weird stuff I do. None of what I do is weird, unconventional or unusual.

And then it hit me: Doing the basics—the fundamentals—is probably unusual in a field noted for quacks and quick-buck artists. I needed to explain some things to our questioner.

It has been a long, strange journey since I first tried to clean and press the Sears Ted Williams barbell in 1965. I have seen utter nonsense, flat-out lies and enough silliness to make a Monty Python skit. Things that were normal training when I first started lifting have now become reinvented.

I usually crack out my collection of *Strength and Health* magazines from 1956 to 1985 or pop open John Jesse's *Wrestling Physical Conditioning Encyclopedia* to discover that everything old is new again. I'm not judging anything as good or bad, I'm just saying that everything on the following list can be found in the old magazines and books:

> *Kettlebells*
>
> *Clubbells*

Circuit training

Sandbag training

Gymnastics for bodybuilding

Fighting… in all its forms

As well as every lift, stretch and move ever imagined

Recently, I was told there was a large internet argument (the slap fight of our era) over whether a certain online training program noted for lots of injuries invented the term "squat snatch."

Well, there's a 1950 book by Larry Barnholth on the squat snatch, so I guess truth must always be tested with alternative facts.

The unconventional thinking I have about strength and conditioning is fairly tame. Let's start with two thoughts that probably won't sit well with many people… and they're justified.

First, most people are simply clueless about strength and conditioning. To quote Bill Murray from *Stripes*, "That's a fact, Jack."

Second, most people literally can NOT "hear" what I'm saying when I discuss strength and conditioning.

This will take a moment to explain.

There are words, symbols and phrases that have a single meaning when we use them. These are called "steno" symbols. When you spell steno backward, you start off with "one" and that helps us remember it.

These are words you hear or read and only think of one thing. Contrast it with a word like "bad." Years ago, you could ask somebody if a movie was good. If they responded, "It was bad," you didn't go.

Later, depending on how the word "bad" was inflected, you might leap into your car and drive to the theater. "Bad" could be very, very good… if said a certain way.

I know this isn't helping yet. Hang on.

The word "desk" has one meaning. If we're on a beach and beautiful person walks past and I say, "Wow, s(he) is sooooo desk," you would ask for further clarification.

Answering by waving my hands and saying, "You know, desk!" probably won't help.

And, now, to my point: Since the publication of Arnold's *The Education of a Bodybuilder*, weightlifting has a steno symbol.

> *Split training*
>
> *Arm day/leg day/back day (I call this Frankenstein's Monster's Training—you're a collection of body parts)*
>
> *Pump up the muscles*
>
> *Protein six times a day from plastic containers (sold to you by your trainer)*
>
> *Whoever dies with the biggest casket wins*
>
> *No pain, no gain*

None of that's remotely true in the world of strength and conditioning. Yet, when I see high school athletes or the football players on Last Chance U exercise, they look like they're using the protocols off the pages of *Muscle and Fantasy* magazine.

Of course, we have a saying for this kind of development:

Looks like Tarzan, plays like Jane.

The former strength coach of the Chicago Bears and all-around great Olympic lifter, Clyde Emrich, said this to Paul Young:

"I feel that there is too much bodybuilding in strength training. Bodybuilding is fine for bodybuilding. But if you're going to perform on the field, you'd better train in a manner that complements this. This is why your multi-joint movements and explosive lifts are the best. Bodybuilding has some application for rehabilitation, but your multi-joint athletic lifts should be your foundation.

"If bodybuilding was the correct way to train for sports, you would see a lot of bodybuilders on the fields and courts. And you don't see that. This is not to knock bodybuilding, but if you're going to be asked to perform as an athlete, you'd better train as an athlete."

The most unconventional idea I have in my head is actually Orthodox thinking… but we have to fight the steno symbol that all lifting is bodybuilding.

All lifting is NOT bodybuilding.

Athletes need to train like athletes. Athletes need:

> *Appropriate strength*
>
> *Appropriate conditioning*
>
> *Appropriate mobility and flexibility*

Usually, I just say, "Enough is enough; more is just more." Athletes need to spend time on strategy, tactics, situations, skills, drills, recovery and appropriate tension, arousal and heart rate.

The same year Arnold wrote his book, we began the geological period known as the "Montage Era." It started with Rocky and has just gone downhill from there. Every sports film has that five-minute sequence of everybody sweating, huffing and puffing and finishing with a high five that ends racial and financial divides and leads them to victory.

Somehow sweating and running up and down stadium steps— albeit with a high five—leads to superior athletic performance.

Your mileage may vary.

My unconventional idea makes me wonder why "all of this" has to be done. I know an athlete of mine who went off to compete at a Division I university. The athlete showed me the training program, and my head exploded.

Since I'm responsible for half of this athlete's DNA, I felt I needed to ask the key question:

"How many rabbits are you chasing?"

There's an old saying: If you chase two rabbits, you go hungry. The program had hypertrophy, mobility, flexibility (two kinds… of course!), plyometrics, Olympic lifts, power lifts, circuits, agility and… you get the point.

When I was in the spring of my senior year as a discus thrower at Utah State University, my strength program was this:

> *Snatch*
>
> *Clean*

On heavy days, I'd snatch just under 300 and clean just under 400 pounds. That workout and a lot of discus throwing lead me to throw the discus far.

I was chasing one rabbit.

I always get hammered online about my list of fundamental human movements: push, pull, hinge, squat, loaded carries. Everything else we call "the sixth movement." Most of the sixth movement is climbing and crawling, but other people lose their minds because I don't include lunges.

Lunges, for God's sake.

I have yet to hear an athlete take me aside and tell me, "Coach, the difference this year is the lunges."

But here's my point. It's just "more." We just sent Igor to the cemetery to find more parts.

You can certainly disagree if you can disagree with some level of knowledge, experience and tact.

Cueing and Coaching—
Appropriate Information at the Appropriate Time

Watching a young coach or trainer struggle teaching something basic is often illuminating. I have total empathy—I've been there. My enthusiastic efforts teaching the Olympic lifts for the first time in 1979 were filled with information, ideas and insight.

I probably told my poor first athletes the entire history of the sport, the importance of each and every stop along the path of the bar, and deep discussions about the various schools of approaching high-level success. I used to teach like a fire hose: plenty of pressure and information at a rate that no one could even take a sip.

I got better.

To help young coaches, I now use two simple terms: cueing and coaching. Cueing is the quick code word or reminder. Coaching is named after a vehicle that takes one from here to there. Coaching can be everything from a story to an example to an inspiring talk. Both cueing and coaching are important.

With my Movement Matrix, I break down all the movements I teach, which, as you know, are push, pull, hinge, squat and loaded carry.

Then, I fill in the chart across: isometrics (planks), then strength and hypertrophy moves, then anti-rotation and, at last, ballistics.

Here's my example:

MOVEMENT	PLANKS AS A PROGRAM	STRENGTH TRAINING *LESS THAN 10 REPS* / HYPERTROPHY *15–25 REPS*	ANTI-ROTATION WORK	TRIADS	OLYMPIC LIFTS
PUSH	PUPPs Plank	(Bench) Press Pushup	One-arm Bench Press One-arm Overhead Press	Push Press/Jerk · Swings · LitviSprints/LitviSleds	Squat Snatch · Clean and Jerk
PULL	Bat Wing	Pullup Row	One-arm TRX Row		
HINGE	Glute Bridge with AB Hold	Hip Thrust Rack DLs Goad Bag Swing	**Hill Sprints** **Stadium Steps** Skipping Bounding High Knee Work		
SQUAT	Goblet Squats 6-point Rocks	Double KB Front Squat The Full Squat Family	**Bear Hug Carries** Bear Crawls Bear Hug Carries with Monster Walk		
LOADED CARRY	Farmer's Walk Horn Walk	Prowler Car Push	One-arm Carries: **Suitcase Carry** Waiter Walk Rack Walk		

On the far right, I have the squat snatch and squat clean and jerk. It took me a while to figure out that not everyone can O lift on the first day they attempt to lift weights.

With the Movement Matrix, I have basically 37 exercises I teach. Obviously, this doesn't include every correction, regression and progression, but it's close. Once I had done this chart, I spent the next few years coming up with cues.

It took a while.

Cues are short points coaches yell to emphasize the most coachable movement points during an exercise. Often, it's not much. Most of the time, I only allow, "Go-go-go!" Now, if you have time, as in a plank or isometric, you can say more:

PUPP (Pushup Position Plank)

Hands: "Grip and rip"

Armpits: "Crush the grapes and make wine"

Knees: "Squeeze the knees"

Bat Wings

"Thumbs in pits"

"Elbows together"

"Hold… Squeeze!"

Glute Bridge

"Butt and belly"

"Knees" (use the Glute Loop)

"Pull down" (ab hold… pull band to zipper)

Goblet Squat

"Push the knees out with the elbows"

"Slide between the legs"

"Stay tall"

Farmer Walks

"Stay tall"

"Walk the Line" (sing it like Johnny Cash)

With the family of planks, two things emerge. First, if you have time—up to two minutes—you can engage the human brain more. In the O lifts, I suggest stapling your lips closed during the movement. When I throw the discus, as my right foot comes off the ground, I deliver the discus in about one second. There's no time there to use the brain to do anything but foul things up.

In other words, shut up during ballistic movements.

Second, note that two of the cues are present throughout all training programs.

"Squeeze."

"Stand tall."

These represent two of the three great lessons of loaded carry work, especially the bear hug family. "Squeeze" builds that "anaconda strength," the inner tube. I read an article years ago from an Olympic hammer champion, who tried to explain that true athletic strength was building up internal pressure. He described it like a bicycle inner tube you need to learn to pump up for performance.

Next, "stand tall" reminds us of the "arrow strength" we strive to build. In many sports, there comes an instant when the athlete blocks the movement to transfer all the speed into the implement or ball. It's that ability to turn the body into a brick wall… or an arrow… that makes for superior performance.

Anaconda and arrow strength come from my understanding of Stu McGill's important work in explaining hammer and stone. Hammer is the power generated by slamming the feet into the ground and being propelled upward. Stone is the body staying rigid so all the energy goes up, not lost in the various soggy tremors of the body.

As a strength coach, I can keep you "stoned" by the loaded carry family, planks and deadlifts.

When it comes to the rest of the movements, I believe you need to have cue words to get people to focus on the big keys.

Anaconda Work (bear hugs)

"Squeeze!"

Swings

"Hinge, plank"

Litvi-Family (after the "drop")

"Go, Go, Go"

Snatch and Clean from the Hang

"Slide"

"Up"

"Jump"

Overhead Ballistics

Push Press: "Dip, snap"

Push Jerk: "Dip, slap"

Jerk: "Dip, stomp"

Cues need to be simple. Cues need to be used by every coach in the same way. Cues should be very narrow and repeatable.

After the movement is finished and the weight or implement has been returned safe and sound, allow the athlete a moment to regain clarity and THEN coach. Explain the bow and arrow, the ground force concept, the angles, grooves and trajectories.

Coaching is often simply applying the best regression, correction or progression for the person. Although we stay with the basic movements, we're constantly searching for the appropriate next challenge. We want beautiful movement—we want mastery.

For mastery, cue constantly and coach appropriately.

Further Down the Road with Easy Strength

INTRODUCTION TO EASY STRENGTH

The following is an attempt to explain a strength program for athletes. Many athletes need to get stronger (obviously), but don't have the time to train like a strength sport athlete, AND train for the specific sport.

Easy strength takes care of this quality: strength.

Oddly, some of the best results of this program have come from older, advanced trainees (not athletes, but experienced trainers) who have said, literally, "I just wanted to see what could happen."

Easing up for eight weeks and focusing on just one quality seems to be the answer to a lot of problems.

The emails are often incredulous rants about how "obvious this all is." I hope so. The key is doing the program, not missing reps and basically doing the same thing over and over for 40 workouts.

The acquisition of strength is like learning to type better. To get better at typing, you type. You don't push harder to type better, nor do you guzzle energy drinks. You type.

To get stronger, sometimes you just need to "show up and lift" for 40 workouts.

As always, the secret to success is to "show up."

EASY STRENGTH

"Easy strength" is a term first used, I believe, by Steve Baccari. I wouldn't be surprised if I heard it from Marty Gallagher too, as great minds think alike.

It's odd to explain this to people who just read fitness magazines and online insanity, but strength is actually an easy quality to improve. Here: Lift weights.

I only joke a bit.

Like flexibility, strength is "learned" by the body. That's why so many things work. When I was stuck as an Olympic lifter recovering from heavy cleans, Dave Turner had me do a few weeks of isometrics at the exact spot where I struggled in the front squat.

"Instantly," over about six weeks, I never had an issue again. My nervous system learned what to do.

The problem with going to failure or training with insanity—I can't make this idiocy up—is that the body gets tired, but it seems not to learn how to get stronger.

First the nervous system figures it out, then the load begins to climb. It seems the body has a discussion about all this additional load and the hormones kick in with, to use Robb Wolf's lovely term, "the hormonal cascade." The body grows and adapts in interesting ways.

Easy Strength is a simple system of repeating the lifts we want to improve with lighter but progressive loads. The idea is to make the heavier loads feel easy.

I learned this same concept from John Powell, a former world record holder in the discus. One day, he told me a secret that changed my career.

John's insight was simple: Once you throw 200 feet after training for years and doing all the right things, how do you get to 201?

More?

More what?

Instead, John argued that rather than try to force that 100% effort higher, focus on 80%.

How easy can you throw 160? Well, it's ridiculously easy to throw 160... so easy, you throw 180. No, he said... 160. Suddenly, as everything eases off, and maybe you focus on throwing into a bucket or trash can at 160, it becomes even easier.

Soon, your 80% is maybe 165 or 170. Maybe—John argued—your 100% isn't 200 anymore... it's farther. Losing your mind trying to MAKE yourself improve is far less efficient than simply prodding your easy efforts up.

This is Easy Strength in a nutshell. Never miss a lift. If you miss, it was too heavy. Never strain. Never snort, nor scream.

Take it easy.

When the load feels too light, go heavier.

That sentence is what most people miss from the Easy Strength program. Let's begin the adventure of explaining how to do the program, and maybe learn some more things on the way.

Bus Bench and Park Bench

If you regularly read my work, you know the concept of the benches: a bus bench and a park bench.

The concept of park bench and bus bench comes from the late Archbishop George Niederauer. He described this with prayers, but it works great with weightlifting too. He said, "There are certain kinds of prayers where you want a result."

Those are bus bench prayers. When you sit on a bus bench, you wait for and expect the bus to arrive.

Archbishop Niederauer also had what he called "the park bench" concept. When you sit on a park bench, you have almost no expectations except to enjoy the sun for a few minutes and maybe watch a squirrel or two.

The bench looks the same. Different expectations.

In weightlifting, fitness and most sports, we have programs based on both ideas. Park bench workouts are "punch the clock" workouts. There's no peak. Do some work without expectation.

Bus bench programs are peaking programs. They're all the "do this" programs. There's a result you're aiming for—it's all sketched out, and you follow the plan.

Both types of programs have a purpose. It can be nice to cycle both styles throughout a year. Selecting a bus bench program two to four times per year and filling the gaps with park bench workouts is a good approach.

Easy Strength is a workout that's actually both. You expect to get stronger, yes.

But, it just arrives.

The Hangover Rule

I learned a great lesson at dining tables and bars: Some of the most amazing feats in track and field history have come from less-than-stellar stories. This rule, the hangover rule, doesn't happen in the vertical jumps—high jump and pole vault—because the athletes know what they're about to do.

But, very often… more than you think… an amazing performance comes on the day after an evening of too much fun. The athlete slumps onto the field and tries to find a place to nap, expecting nothing, save to show up and keep the promise of competing.

An odd thing happens: The warmups don't feel great, but something "good" is going on. Maybe the first efforts are a bit sluggish, but the distances or speed are very good.

Not long after, the mark is yelled out to the crowd, and the crowd goes crazy.

It's a new world record! When I first heard about this, the storyteller added the lovely image of puking into some rose bushes as he walked up to the facility.

Why does this happen? Why does someone do so well when hung over or (fill in the blank)?

Because that's the way it works.

I've been with people who have elaborate plans about meeting the "love of my life," yet the story never unfolds like the plan.

Memorize that.

I think Easy Strength works for this same reason: You don't expect much, so you just get in the work.

And, then, like meeting the love of your life at a party where she's being set up with your friend (as happened to me, for example), the magic happens.

I wished peaking worked more often. But, it usually doesn't.

If it did, everyone would do well at the Nationals... at least seasonal bests. That rarely happens. I'll discuss peaking a bit—after we get a sense of the full preparation of the Easy Strength protocol.

The Beginning of the Modern Easy Strength

Years ago, when I first met Pavel Tsatsouline, he challenged me to do a "40-day workout." I followed his simple instructions to a T.

"For the next 40 workouts, pick five lifts. Do them every workout. Never miss a rep, in fact, never even get close to struggling. Go as light as you need to go, and don't go over 10 reps for any of the movements in a workout. It's going to seem easy. When the weights feel light, simply add more weight."

I did exactly as he said. On the 22nd workout, alone in my garage gym, I broke my lifetime best incline bench press record—300 for a single. Without a spotter, in a frozen garage, I benched 315 for a double. All the other lifts went through the roof, and I'm as amazed now as I was then.

It's too easy. In fact, it's so easy, I've had to break it down into literally dozens of pages of articles to make it as simple as possible! And, the more I try to simplify it, honestly, the more lost some people become thinking about the program.

I'm not entirely convinced I'm a genius, but somebody has to prove to me why I followed those simple instructions so easily and vast hordes of trainers can't seem to follow the concept without the obvious answer that I have an unrivaled intelligence.

Or, perhaps, I just can follow simple rules.

EASIER STRENGTH

So, I came up with Easier Strength. I didn't want to do this, but I was exhausted explaining to people that, "three sets of three, adding weight each time it feels easy" meant to do, "three sets of three, adding weight each time it feels easy."

My frustrations led to even more clarity.

Let's start with an advanced experienced trainer who has never done any loaded carries. In three weeks, I will be a genius, as the farmer walks alone will change everything.

There are a few rules before we begin:

1. Never miss a rep!

2. Follow the "Rule of 10" for the appropriate lifts for an advanced lifter. Keep the total number of reps at 10 or fewer.

Advanced athlete's warmups

10–15 goblet squats (ss many or few sets as you want or need)

75 swings or hinge variations (sets of 10–25—really grease that hinge movement)

Mobility as needed

Easy Strength for an experienced lifter

Week One

Mon **(1)** 2x5, Tues **(2)** 2x5, Wed **(3)** 5–3–2, Thu off, Fri **(4)** 2x5, Sat **(5)** 2x5, Sun off

Week Two

Mon **(6)** 2x5, Tues **(7)** 6 singles, Wed **(8)** 1x10, Thu off, Fri **(9)** 2x5, Sat **(10)** 5–3–2, Sun off

LIFTS

Press movement: You might decide to change the lifts every two weeks—same, but different. Flat bench press, incline bench press and military press can be exchanged for each other after every two-week block. Or just stick with one, like I did the first time.

Pull movement: Pullups or chinups (or, yes, neutral-grip pullups) seem to work better than anything else. I've often just done six singles the first few days to practice the movement.

Hinge movement: There are two options here, depending on need: either pick a deadlift variation (and rotate it every two weeks, for example, thick-bar deadlifts, snatch-grip deadlifts, clean-grip deadlifts, orthodox deadlifts, Jefferson lifts or hack squats) or do kettlebell swings in the 75–100 range. But, you have to be good at swings.

Many people have found that doing BOTH a deadlift and a swing works wonders. After trying this myself, I think it works the best. At least, until I try something else.

Loaded carry: Vary the distance EVERY time, and probably the load if you can.

You might notice I haven't listed the squat. I've been doing this programming for nearly two decades, and just can't get the squat to work. Squatting is great, but maybe not here.

Here's what works with Easy Strength:

> *Vertical press*
>
> *Vertical pull (pullups and variations)*
>
> *Deadlift variations*
>
> *Swings and loaded carries (the swing in the warmup is plenty for most people)*
>
> *Ab wheel*

The swings and ab wheel are the salt and pepper; the other three are the main course.

If you need to know the squat movements, here you go (and I'd love you to succeed doing these!):

Squat movement: Front squats, back squats, overhead squats, Zercher squats or safety squats are all fine.

The Easier Strength Workouts

Let's take a look at the specifics. The workouts look like this:

Week One

> Mon (1) 2x5, Tues (2) 2x5, Wed (3) 5–3–2, Thu off,
> Fri (4) 2x5, Sat (5) 2x5, Sun off

Week Two

> Mon (6) 2x5, Tues (7) 6 singles, Wed (8) 1x10, Thu off,
> Fri (9) 2x5, Sat (10) 5–3–2, Sun off

Two sets of five: It should be easy and be like your second or third warmup lift in a typical workout. The idea, the "secret," is to get THIS workout to feel easier and easier!

Five-three-two: Five reps with your 2x5 weight; add weight for three, then a solid double. Make the double!!!

Six singles: I don't care how you do this, but add weight each set. No misses!

One set of 10: The day after six singles, do a very light load for 10 easy "tonic" reps.

EXAMPLE WORKOUT FOR AN EXPERIENCED LIFTER

Monday, Day One

> *Incline bench press:*
> 165 for five reps, 165 for five reps (300 max single)

Thick bar deadlifts:
185 for five reps, 185 for five reps (265 max single)

Pullups:
Two sets of five

Farmer walks:
105 with each hand, 100 meters out and back (three stops)

Ab wheel:
Five reps

Day two can be heavier or lighter depending on mood and feel. The important thing is to show up and get in the movements. If one day is too hard and compromises the next day, that's fine as long as you lighten the load and continue getting the reps without compromising speed.

Day three should begin with the five-rep number from the usual 2x5 workout, then add weight for three, and finally add weight for two. Be sure to get the double.

Most people on the Easy Strength program find this workout is the test for how things are progressing. The weights begin to fly up on the double—and that's good, but stop there. Remember, this is a long-term approach to getting strong. Don't keep testing yourself. Save the big effort for, well, never.

Days four and five are the most confusing days. Again, the load on the bar depends on how you feel. If the efforts feel easy and light, nudge the load up. Here's the secret (again): The goal of this program is gently raise your efforts (load) on the easy days so the bar feels light. If you start lifting a weight, say 205 at one effort level, and in a few weeks you're lifting 245 at the same perceived effort and speed, you're stronger.

After a day of rest, day six will feel easy, and it should be. Get the reps in.

Day seven has a simple rule: You will do six singles adding weight EACH rep. It can be five pounds or 50, depending on how each single feels. It's NOT a max effort on the last set—it's the sixth single. If the loads feel heavy, just add five pounds. If the bar is flying, add more.

For people who come from the tradition of "smashing the face on the wall," day seven is confusing. Your goal is to determine the load by how the weight feels. If it pops up and feels light, toss on the plates. If it doesn't, respect today, and realize you're going to have plenty of opportunities to get stronger in the future.

Day eight is a "tonic" day—the way we used to use the term. Go really light and just enjoy 10 repetitions. It can be as light as 40% of max (or lighter if you feel like it), and just use the movement to unwind after yesterday's heavy attempts.

Day nine is often the day when people see the reasoning behind the program. This is the day when the weights seem to be far too easy. That's the sign of progress in this program. I remember actually thinking I misloaded the bar, and I had to double-check my math because the bar seemed to be far too light to be right.

Day ten is often the day when people test themselves a little. This can be fine as long as you feel like going after it. Again, don't miss.

WEEK THREE: TIME FOR A CHANGE?

Depending on the person, some will need variation. Some won't. I offer three ideas for week three.

Week Three, Option One

The original program Pavel designed demanded that I repeat weeks one and two for three additional times. It worked well. By week five, I was a machine on the lifts and broke lifetime personal records, smashing my incline bench press record by 15 pounds (doing it for two reps, not just a single) and crushing my old thick-bar deadlift record (from 265 to 315). This is a staggering improvement in such a short time. Option one is to simply keep on keeping on.

Week Three, Option Two

I like this more for most athletes. You make small changes to the movements, from bench press to incline bench press, thick-bar deadlift to snatch-grip deadlift and pullup to chinup. This is Pavel's "same, but different" approach. The small changes keep enthusiasm high for the entire eight weeks.

Week Three, Option Three

I have a few athletes doing this now, and I believe (maybe "hope" is a better word) this is a better option for speed and power athletes. It's both a deload week, and week filled with more metabolic challenges. Have a look:

Day One

Push press or push jerk, five sets of two (Rule of 10), adding weight each set, is a great workout.

"Lift and offs" (used to be Litvinovs): After doing a hinge or a squat movement, either sprint, sled or prowler immediately after finishing the first movement. In a gym setting, this can be difficult, but I've done this outside with great success with just a kettlebell and a hill.

In a gym setting, squats followed quickly by prowlers can be amazing. Just don't pause between the movements.

Day Two

Left hand only!

- *Waiter walk*
- *Suitcase walk*
- *Single-arm front squat (kettlebells are best)*

- *Suitcase deadlift*
- *One-arm row on the* TRX *(or suitable device)*
- *One-arm bench press*

Reps, sets, load, time and every other factor "depend." The idea is to push the stability and symmetry muscles and movements. There's an odd metabolic hit to these moves as one sweats a lot more than expected with these.

For example, this can be done with a single kettlebell in a park (which is wonderful, by the way), and the athlete can challenge various aspects of training. You'll get a good workout while also practicing mastery of body position and dynamics.

Doing just one side also frees up the mind a little. It's pretty obvious what you'll be doing in a few days, so you can experiment a bit and play the edges of tension and relaxation as you train.

Day Three

Push press or push jerk, five sets of two (Rule of 10), adding weight each set, is a great workout.

"Lift and offs" (used to be Litvinovs): After doing a hinge or a squat movement, either sprint, sled or prowler immediately after finishing the first movement. In a gym setting, this can be difficult, but I've done this outside with great success with just a kettlebell and a hill.

In a gym setting, squats followed quickly by prowlers can be amazing, just don't pause in between the movements.

Day Four

Right arm only!

- *Waiter walk*
- *Suitcase walk*

- *Single-arm front squat (kettlebells are best)*
- *Suitcase deadlift*
- *One-arm row on the TRX (or suitable device)*
- *One-arm bench press.*

At the beginning of week four, mix up the variations of the basic movements (push, pull, hinge, squat, loaded carry), and progress using the same rep-and-set template as in weeks one and two.

After finishing the program (weeks one and two repeated four times total; option three would be a 12-week program), fully assess mobility, basic strength levels and the program vis-à-vis your goals.

I suggest maybe a Functional Movement Screen and blood tests too, if costs aren't an issue.

Realistic Reps
and Simple Ideas Most of the Time

As much as I love Easy Strength, after two 40-day courses, it's time for a change. I'm generally a fan of mild changes. If you use the workout generator on *danjohnuniversity.com,* we take care of it for you. If not, let's review the basics of something I call "realistic reps."

One of the real issues in modern training is clearing all the junk from people's heads when it comes to reps and sets. There seems to be this belief that the human body has gone through some massive changes since Thomas DeLorme published *Progressive Resistance Exercise* and Theodor Hettinger wrote *The Physiology of Strength.*

These two texts bookend much of my knowledge of the field. These are authors who studied lots of people, tried different ideas and came to some brilliant conclusions. I often summarize Hettinger's work at my talks:

- The calves can increase in strength 6% a week; the glutes 4%; the triceps 3%; and the biceps 2%.

- Men are stronger than women. In tests, some parts of women are 55% as strong as men (forearm extensors), but in the hip area it rises to 80%. (Teaching girls to shot put: you will notice that they can glide or spin on day one, but it might take a bit of time to get the proper release—that 55% is real!)

- Strength peaks in the late 20s, maintains for a long time and gradually declines, especially in untrained people.

- It's easier to train in the summer. Vitamin D might help that too.

- Injecting testosterone seems to make everybody train better for a long time.

That last point explains why so many idiotic programs can work even though they break the laws of reason and experience.

If you use the words "sets," "reps," or even practice "progressive resistance," you need to thank a brave WWII doctor named Thomas DeLorme. In 1979, I was told that no one has ever proved to find a better training protocol than DeLorme's famous three sets of ten (or eight).

Terry and Jan Todd, along with Jason Shurley, wrote extensively on DeLorme's influence. They sum his work as:

"In the latter years of the Second World War, the number of American servicemen who had sustained orthopedic injuries was overwhelming the nation's military hospitals. The backlog of patients was partly because of the sheer number of soldiers involved in the war effort, but it was exacerbated by rehabilitation protocols that required lengthy recovery times.

"In 1945, an army physician, Dr. Thomas L. DeLorme experimented with a new rehabilitation technique. DeLorme had used strength training to recover from a childhood illness and reasoned that such heavy training would prove beneficial for the injured servicemen.

"DeLorme's new protocol consisted of multiple sets of resistance exercises in which patients lifted their 10-repetition maximum. DeLorme refined the system by 1948 to include three progressively heavier sets of 10 repetitions, and he referred to the program as 'Progressive Resistance Exercise.' The high-intensity program was markedly more successful than older protocols and was quickly adopted as the standard in both military and civilian physical therapy programs.

"In 1951, DeLorme published the text *Progressive Resistance Exercise: Technic and Medical Application*, which was widely read by other physicians and medical professionals. The book, and DeLorme's academic publications on progressive resistance exercise, helped legitimize strength training and played a key role in laying the foundation for the science of resistance exercise."

Oddly, today many people forget DeLorme… or have never heard of him and his pioneering work.

I frame much of my training from the insights of Hettinger and DeLorme. When I talk about reps and sets, I feel like I stand on firm ground.

You already know I break training basically into five movements. You can do more, but I should be allowed to ask, "Why?"

When it comes to the basics, the push, pull and squat numbers should have the same weekly volume. These are the hypertrophy, mobility, flexibility and power moves—keep them all at the same volume number.

That challenge drives most people crazy. Usually, people send me programs with 200 pushes a week, 50 pulls and 10 squats. Nope.

I want something like 75 across the board. If you did five sets of five, three days a week of bench press, pullup, front squat for two weeks, followed by military press, row and back squat, I could sleep well knowing you did some real work.

For the push, pull and squat, you can play around with three sets of eight, five sets of three or whatever gets you into that 15–25 or 30 range for total reps. If you compete, you might want to do three sets of three or five sets of two, but most of us thrive with DeLorme's numbers.

With the hinge, I have to ask what you're doing. If you're doing kettlebell swings, somewhere between 75 reps and 500 reps is a good workout. For a long time, I thought 250 swings was sustainable, but I've lowered that a bit—75 swings is five sets of 15, and that's a good warmup or even workout. Adding more heavy swings is an idea, but 125 seems to be the number that's repeatable… and doable.

But the deadlift is also a hinge. Consider this: 75 swings with a 24-kilo kettlebell is laudable, but how does that relate to few reps with 500–600 pounds? I dunno!

With loaded carries, be sure to vary everything every day. I have some odd workouts with loaded backpacks, dragging a sled, carrying farmer bars with mini-bands around my ankles. It's fun. Simply carrying a weight in one hand and alternating it back and forth as you walk is excellent and a few quality sprints with a sled are fine too.

Whatever. Just change it up every time.

OPTIONAL READ FOR ELITE ATHLETES OR THOSE WITH TRAINING GAPS

Now, the workout doesn't necessarily have to go in this order:

Warmups

Push

Pull

Hinge

Squat

Loaded carries (walk/run/sprint under load)

Correctives

In fact, I think the real insight of the past 10 years for me was understanding the role of perceived strengths and weaknesses by the athlete in the training system. It has changed the way I view programming.

Simply, divide the TIME involved in the workout in half. Yes, this will involve math.

If each day is an hour workout (about right for most strength programs), the total time for strength training in the above template is five hours a week. Elite athletes can train in the weight room up to 10 hours a week, but that would mean actual athletic training would be upward of 40 hours a week including film, games, and all the rest—and, "all the rest" can be a lot of time for a professional.

My simple method is this: Divide the time in half. The first half of every training session would be devoted to the perceived strengths the athlete has in the five basic human movements. This time would also include mobility and flexibility correctives.

It's an aspect of human nature I've come to acknowledge: If I reward you with what you do well, you'll do the little things like correctives.

The other half of the training time will be dedicated to weaknesses or omissions. Since the athlete will be learning new skills and movements, all energy has to be devoted to mastering the new tasks. I remember well learning to squat deep with Dick Notmeyer—every set and rep was stressful physically, mentally and emotionally. Learning to front squat deep flat out hurts!

Some movements, like the warmup movements of the goblet squat, swing and getup, also serve as correctives for many people. If someone is learning the squat, a set of goblet squats between a set of bench presses is quite instructive. It certainly develops the pattern, but it also provides extra time to master the movement.

If you give this an honest try, you'll be amazed at the simplicity of this game-changing tweak.

Correctives can be those kettlebell moves labeled in the warmups, but it also includes any specialized mobility work like we find in the whole corrective library of movements. It can also include foam rolling and general flexibility work too. Instead of resting between sets, you're actively battling your issues.

It doesn't always work perfectly with the available time, as advanced athletes often have few weaknesses in the weight room. But, almost universally, they ignore loaded carries and struggle with squat depth. Finishing a workout with squats and farmer walks or prowlers is exhausting, and we might be better served by resting.

Mix your corrective work between sets. Mix the stuff you haven't been doing throughout the training session.

Remember this great coaching insight: Correct your weaknesses (gaps), but compete with your strengths.

Ideally, soon, you won't have anything to correct.

APPLYING EASY STRENGTH TO SPORTS

Does Easy Strength work? Yes.

So, why don't we have "X" athletes do it?

We do; they improve quickly, and everyone is happy!

How about "Y" athletes?

Hmmm, well, you know… it depends!

The Quadrants for Strength Coaches

Years ago, Pavel asked me a simple question, "What is the role of the strength coach?"

That's easy: to coach strength. People arrive, we train, they get stronger and... we're all happy.

"Yes, but," he went on, "what's the *impact* of the strength coach?"

Now that's a completely different question.

I understood the answer on many levels. Sometimes, the more experience one has, the harder it is to sum all the conflicting and contradictory thoughts.

Years ago, I read that a young girl raised her hand and asked an expert in nuclear warfare, "Wouldn't it be simpler if we just destroyed all the weapons?"

The expert covered his head with his hands and said, "If only it was that simple."

My task was simple: to discern the impact of the strength coach so we could "instantly" describe the relative importance of strength coaching on the journey toward specific goals.

Every so often, I rediscover the yellow legal pad where I laid out my doodles, pictures, graphs and geometric shapes attempting to explain the impact of the strength coach. I went through a lot of ideas, but the thing that kept me sane was a simple insight.

Here it is: Only certain people need chase the biggest numbers in the weightroom. They have the genetics, the geography and the goal of snatching or deadlifting or squatting more weight than anyone on this planet has ever done. They have a singular vision… a single goal.

The rest of us need to become relatively stronger for a goal, but not as strong (or as fast… or as fill in the blank) as these people in that narrow band of chasing a single quality.

Some people need a LOT of qualities at a relatively high level. Others just need a little exposure to things, and another group needs to get fairly strong and still chase a high level of performance in another field (literally, "in a field" in many cases).

I shaped my idea into four quadrants with the X axis rising up to the limits of human abilities and the Y axis the number of qualities people chasing this goal would need.

Quadrant One represents lots of qualities, all at a low level. This would be physical education in youth.

Quadrant Two needs lots of qualities at a relatively high level. These are collision sports and occupations.

Quadrant Three is a few (two or three) qualities at a comparatively low level. This is most of us. Yet, oddly, it's also the bulk of the Olympic sports.

Quadrant Four is one (or perhaps two) qualities at the highest levels of human performance. Think about the 100-meter sprint, the Olympic lifts and single-lift powerlifters.

Quadrant One

There is something magical about youth. Maybe we can say, there WAS something magical about youth. As a child, the best part of Christmas were the huge tubes of cardboard Mom would give me after she used the last bit of wrapping paper.

Those tubes would become cannons to shoot at the enemy warships, rifle barrels to fight for freedom and swords to keep the Three Musketeer enemies at bay. We climbed trees to snipe our foes, climbed under porches and generally made nuisances of ourselves. These tools, in my family, became part of survival fighting in America's various wars.

Today, we see playgrounds being denuded of monkey bars, swings, teeter totters and all variety and kind of playground mischief. But there's a cost of all that "safety"—the cost in learning the basics of human experience.

George Hebert warned us about this a century ago. He argued that there are 10 tools for survival that can literally save us as we move through life.

> *Pursuit: walk, run, crawl*
>
> *Escape: climb, balance, jump, swim*
>
> *Attack: throw, lift, fight*

I learned them all as a child and, if I may, I'd like to include two more: tumbling (or break-falling) and riding a bicycle.

There's an old story about a young man who goes off to study theology. On the way home after years of study, he needs to get across a river, so he hires a boatman. Halfway across the river, the boatman asks, "What did you learn in school?"

"Important things about the universe, life and everything."

"Ah. Did you learn to swim?"

"No, only important things."

"Ah. Too bad. The boat is sinking."

Quadrant One is the crucial period of life when we learn integrity with the environment. We learn the vertical environment by climbing and crawling over things. We learn the horizontal environment by crawling under things, skipping over stuff and generally running amok.

These are life lessons. If you didn't learn Hebert's skills as a child, when will you?

Training in Quadrant One

One of the things that turns me off is going into a hotel (usually exhausted) and seeing a bunch of kids dressed in $1,000 uniforms and gear sticking their fingers into the free breakfast buffet. These kids belong to "elite" teams—and they'll be the first to tell you.

Mom and Dad write checks so Junior or Sissy can play. In my world, people pay my people to play… not the other way around. Mom and Dad are always convinced that this elite team is their child's ticket to education.

The ticket to free education is education. It's doing well in classes, being involved and pursuing the noble ideals of a liberal education: the education of a free person (not a mule). It's writing and reading and creating.

If the parents simply took the money spent on these sports and buried it in a coffee can in the backyard, the child's education fund would be much further ahead.

David Epstein's book, *Range*, does a masterful job deciphering this for us. The 10,000-hour rule works ONLY in areas of instant feedback and the ability to clump (or cluster) patterns. It's mastering classical instruments, chess and golf. It doesn't work in many other areas… if any.

Early specialization doesn't take into account the real two keys to sports success: genetics and geography, my summary of Epstein's first book, *The Sports Gene*.

I was blessed as an athlete because my folks didn't allow me to do organized sports outside of church ball. But, I played sports probably six or seven hours a day. We didn't hydrate; we drank out of the hose. We didn't warm up because we were too busy playing. We cooled down when Mom yelled it was time for dinner or it got too dark.

Yes, I miss it.

What should our little ones be doing? First, let's remember that clue from George Herbert:

> **Pursuit:** *walk, run, crawl*
>
> **Escape:** *climb, balance, jump, swim*
>
> **Attack:** *throw, lift, fight*

Tim Anderson's *Original Strength* is based, in part, on retraining this gap in most people's lives.

Playgrounds and swimming pools are the habitat of the future greats. Now, the "attack" options should probably have some training, but all we used was Ted William's training manual, and then just figured out lifting for ourselves.

This "look at the picture method" is literally what everyone else my age did for lifting education. My mom and dad taught me to box, so maybe I had other advantages that others didn't have.

As I told you, I added two things to Herbert's list: tumbling or break-falling and riding a bicycle. I tell people this often: The most dangerous thing in the home for me is the floor (or stairs). At my age, the floor is a killer. The lessons I learned in judo still protect me anytime I slip or snag something.

Bike riding? When I was at that Emergency Prep Conference and the speaker noted that you always need to be able to go 90 miles from your home no matter what the issue might be… from nuclear to biological to earthquake, she drilled in that universally, 90 miles keeps you safe.

I always have basic bikes (no gears, coaster brakes) that can get me and my family 90 miles. We haven't trained this challenge, but we can do it. We can carry them over fallen overpasses or whisk around rubble. With that 72-hour emergency backpack, we can, at least, get away. What happens next… well, I don't want to think about that.

These are life lessons. Herbert's list is difficult to learn later in life. But it's all life-saving stuff.

And… a lot of fun.

Quadrant Two

Sadly, everyone loves to read and perhaps try to follow the training programs of fighters, NFL football players, Navy SEALs and Special Operations people. And… they can't.

Quadrant Two is the realm of collision sports and collision occupations. There may be 100 qualities needed to play in the NFL, from size and speed to the moment-to-moment tactical changes in technique within the rules. It can take a decade to develop the tool kit.

I once explained the basic commando as being a person with a B+ grade in 100 classes. They're not the best at everything, but amazingly good at a lot of things. If you're 22 and NOT in the Navy or in an elite Division I football program, your chances of being a SEAL or NFL player are practically, without divine intervention… nil.

The impact of the strength coach on collision sports and occupations is "it depends." Sometimes, the best answer in the world is "it depends."

Clearly, increasing strength tends to make most people a bit more resilient and more useful. I think many people WANT to be called at night when there's a flat tire, a broken water main or someone with uncontrollable vomiting.

These people are strong and resilient. The weightroom can make them stronger.

In truth, we could have the best facilities, the best coaches and the hardest working cadre of people in the world and still lose. Sometimes, talent just outshines training. And, in total candor, in warfare, the enemy has a vote.

Bad things happen.

Yes, the strength coach can impact the Quadrant Two person. The strength coach can improve some qualities.

But it doesn't guarantee success.

Training in Quadrant Two

One of the hardest lessons I learned in life is that the barbell (and the whole family of progressive resistance exercises) can do amazing things for us. That little barbell set you bought in 1965 can make you stronger, bigger, leaner and faster.

It's simple stuff. Like Dick Notmeyer told me nearly every day, "He who lifts the heaviest weights gets the strongest."

But, and there's always a but, Dick was talking about getting stronger. "Pound for pound" is basically a lost phrase, but it was a cornerstone of thinking when I was young.

In the mid-1970s, when Jane Fonda and her "go for the burn" videos appeared and Arnold's double-biceps pose became the focus of training, the world embraced lean flanks and big guns as the epitome of strength training. People began to tell us they wanted to look like athletes.

The phrase "Looks like Tarzan, plays like Jane" emerged during this period. Absolutely, this is sexist, but we all know what it means: The decision to "train like a SEAL" or "look like an athlete" is as cosmetic as liposuction or breast augmentation.

I have NOTHING against this. I don't care what your fitness goals are, nor do I really care about how you get there. If you just want to look good… well, bless you.

I know this: You will probably still call me when you need a couch moved up a few flights of stairs.

The issue—the problem—with Quadrant Two is that the normal person often wants to "look like" QII people. It's alluring. It's sexy to want to look like an NFL defensive back or an elite team special operator.

Of course, they don't actually look like the TV and movie star image. Generally, they look like your neighbor… save for the multiple deployments to the Middle East. And, they also have the ability to break into your house, car, boat or airplane, sit quietly for 72 hours staring at one spot, and leave literally everything better after they've used it.

QII is rare air. It's dozens of qualities at a high level. You might not be as fast or as strong as an Olympian, but you're faster and stronger in a dozen areas than even well-trained people. A high-level rugby player is bigger, faster, stronger, leaner and better at nearly everything you will ever attempt.

Training for QII is not *looking like* someone who wants to be in QII. You need to be freakishly strong, not look like someone who's freakishly strong. For endurance, you must endure… not take 40 pictures of yourself looking like someone who endures.

To get strong, you need to lift heavy and lift hard.

To endure, you must slap on a backpack and go for hours or days at a time. It's not a movie shoot. When you get a mission or a play, you must rise up and do the job. It's not Hollywood crap. It's life or death.

I can help you in QII if you want to do collision sports and collision occupations. I can't help you *look like* you do collision sports and collision occupations. You need to get strong.

No one cares what you look like.

It's all about getting the job done.

Quadrant Three

I have lived my life in QIII. Ever since Otis Chandler defied his coach at Stanford, snuck out to lift weights and broke the longest standing record in track and field for the shot put, every thrower knows that lifting is a must. Soon, jumpers and sprinters discovered the weight room and the quick improvements measured with tapes and times.

Percy Cerutty, the Australian distance coach, later showed us that marathoners needed to pull a double-bodyweight deadlift and own a bodyweight press.

In track and field, you practice your event and you lift weights.

There, that's it. That's Quadrant Three. You do your singular event and nudge your strength levels up and, over time and with proper tension and arousal, things go faster, higher and farther.

No, you won't lift at the levels of an elite powerlifter or Olympic lifter, but you'll be oddly stronger than most people you'll ever encounter. Of course, the O lifter and powerlifter don't get measured by tapes and timers, just by load.

Most people, even though I don't necessarily include "everybody else" in the quadrants—basically, it was designed for the role of strength coaches with athletes—should think "QIII" when it comes to goals and goal setting.

For fat loss: Lift weights and cook and eat appropriate meals!

For health and longevity: Have a vigorous social life surrounding quality food and go for a walk.

Generally, QIII is two things. Sure, you need to sleep well and do mobility work and read good books, but discus throwers need to throw the discus and get stronger.

The biggest job of the strength coach is to keep the path that simple: Do this and do that.

"What about that thing I saw on that show... ?"

Slap!!!

Do this and do that.

That's all.

Training in Quadrant Three

There is a great word in falconry: yarak. Yarak is that intense vision a raptor has when it's hungry and hunting. It's the pure focus on one thing… food!

Most of us are in Quadrant Three: We need reasonable amounts of strength, flexibility, mobility and every other "ity" you can think of here.

And, really, most of us only have to worry about one or two things when discussing health, fitness, longevity and performance—if you're in a sport or art. "Don't smoke" and "Wear your seatbelt" are statistically the keys to keeping us around for a while. For fat loss, prepare nutritious meals that are filling and lower in calories and get some form of movement in daily. Certainly, other things work, but these are the keys.

In track and field, you can achieve world class status following Coach Maughan's advice: Do your event four days a week and lift three days a week. He added, "for eight years." Most people miss that last part!

If you embarked on an eight-year journey to fat loss and accumulated 365 days a year plus two extra days on the leap years of some caloric deficit, "magic" would happen.

This is the key to QIII: The magic is the focus on one or two things done daily over a long period of time.

Squirrel!

As we often joke, the problem with QIII is that the moment you begin this journey, your attention will be immediately taken by something new and shiny.

I know this from experience.

Squirrel!

What was I talking about?

Success in QIII is oddly simple: Find the one or two keys to your goal (at most three), and just keep coming back, day in and day out, and doing the basics, the fundamentals, the foundations.

It's that simple: Keep coming back to the basics. Ignore the squirrels!

Quadrant Four

Years ago, an administrator asked me about improving speed for our sports teams. I shared some information written by Barry Ross, a brilliant sprint coach, that seems to go against the norms of training. His sprinters deadlift, then rest for five minutes. They only sprint with speed traps, and when the quality drops, they stop. His sprinters do no slow work at all; they get "in shape" by doing a 15-minute walk three times a week for a month with only one rule: You always have to go a bit farther on each new attempt.

It works.

I wasn't ready for the administrator's reaction: "This is it. We need to do this."

He was extremely excited. He wanted us to drop all of our other strength and conditioning and just follow Ross's program.

I didn't know how to break it to him, so I told him softly: That's the stupidest thing we could do."

Sprinting, especially the 100 meters, is all about one thing, one quality: How fast can you go? Sure, you have to react to the starter's pistol, but there's no need for agility, nor do you worry about collisions.

As much as I love the various programs of Olympic lifters, powerlifters and sprinters, these athletes usually only worry about one quality. Yes, certainly there is a need for flexibility in the O lifts, but in today's rare air of elite lifting, genetics takes care of most of the other qualities. You have to be born to lift and born in a place that supports lifting: genetics and geography.

If your national sport is sprinting, you'll find a lot of sprinters. If O lifting dominates the sports coverage, you live among a lot of O lifters.

Moreover, if you clean and jerk 600 pounds with poor flexibility and bad technique, you still get to be the first person ever to do it.

QIV training is exciting to read about and amazing to watch.

Few people coach these sports well. Without question, some of the lessons we learn from QIV are worth learning. But, they don't apply across the board to sports that demand dozens of qualities. There's more to basketball than blazing fast. There is more to soccer than snatches.

QIV is a one-quality world at the highest level humans can achieve. It's not for everyone.

Training in Quadrant Four

Bill March is one of my heroes. He was not only a world-class bodybuilder, but also one of the strongest men to ever walk this planet. Late in his lifting career, he cleaned and pressed 390 pounds so strictly that people still talk about it 50 years later.

Yes, people have done more, but with help from the legs and a massive lean-back. Bill did 390 with no back bend and with locked-out legs.

Bill trained differently. He was a pioneer of isometric contraction. He drove 115 miles several times a week to work out in a home gym. The workouts lasted 36 seconds.

That's right: 36 seconds.

Three tugs of 12 seconds each—one day in a low position for the push, pull and squat, another day in a medium position and a third in a high position. When he recently explained this program, he made an important point:

He didn't think it was right.

But it was.

That's QIV thinking. To achieve the highest levels the human body has ever achieved, you might not be able to follow the well-worn path. You may have to blaze a new trail.

Barry Ross doesn't allow his sprinters to do anything but go fast—no jogging or slow running. His conditioning workouts are oddly just a series of 12 walks where the athlete tries to go just a bit farther each time. Don't be stupid, and go hard on day one!

When I first heard this, I thought it was crazy. There was no way it could work.

But it did.

The most elite lifters in the world, in all disciplines, continually explore and experiment with ideas and tools no one has ever tried. That's QIV training.

It's a tough lesson. If it works, no matter how crazy it is, it works.

And if it works, it's right.

Easy Strength and the Experienced Athlete

I break everyone into two categories in my book, *Can You Go?*

    Active Athletes (A²)

    Everybody Else (E²)

Originally, though, I used the word "aging" instead of "active." That bothered people.

Here's the deal: If you're over 22 and NOT a professional or at the highest level of your sport, you might never get there. It was tough to write that, but there's some truth there, so I continue to repeat it.

Juri Sedych, still the world record holder in the hammer throw, once told me at lunch that an "elite athlete continues to improve every year."

I looked at my efforts and quietly sobbed to myself.

John Powell, the discus thrower, broke my heart even more. He noted that if you weren't world class within three years of focusing on your sport, you probably would never get there.

That's the best argument I've ever seen against early specialization!

Peaking Programs or Goal Achievement

I don't believe that many athletes can peak, nor do I think most people can achieve goals. It's not that either is impossible, or even improbable; it's simply that most people (and athletes) start off well, then shuffle off into a million directions.

And, like I mentioned earlier, often the records fall while the athlete is hung over... or something else has gone wrong. My best throw during my sophomore year in college was when I arrived late, had to change clothes behind some friendly fans, and competed right after I slipped on my jersey.

My second throw was the best of my life until then. No warmups. No plan. Personal record.

When I work with athletes, it's my job as a strength coach to get them as strong as appropriate. Strength magically tends to make people better at things. As I often say, I'm in my 60s, but I'm still the go-to friend people call when they need a sofa moved.

Training the sport, mastering the tactics and strategies and getting stronger is probably the best way to peak. Absolutely, sleep, digestion—actually elimination is more important on game day—and nutrition will play important roles... obviously.

But what's far more important is NOT screwing things up.

Peaking, then, is often simply staying on the path. The path has been walked so many times, it might seem boring and obvious.

Stay on it anyway!

Let me share my secrets of both peaking and achieving goals.

1. First, realize you're powerless NOT to do something stupid. Accept that. Embrace it. Now, promise yourself the following: The goal is to keep the goal the goal. Anything you add to your plan that's not part of the goal will be the problem. Don't do it.

2. Pieces of paper are cheaper than surgeries. Write out your goals, a specific date to achieve them and a general plan from what has worked in the past and what has worked for others. This is 99% of success in planning.

3. Grab a calendar and make a few big red letter Xs on dates when you know things are coming up. Now you won't be surprised when things come up. Next, take a yellow highlighter and highlight the days with issues. These could be something as simple as school finals or appointments for the dog.

4. Steal other people's paths. There's a ton of information available for anything you might be attempting. Success leaves tracks. Follow them.

5. Assemble the tools, supplies and information needed for correctives. If you're going to use a foam roller in your program, get a foam roller. Allow about 10% of your training time to restorative work, correctives, mobility, flexibility or any kind of stuff you think helps.

6. If you're involved in a sport, 80% of your training time should be doing the activity. For most, 10% of your time should be on developing strength, another 10 on correctives (planned recovery), but the bulk should be on the specific activity.

7. For most situations, the day before competition should be an 80% day (hard to define, but most people have a feel for it), but two days before should be 60%, perhaps even just a warmup. The

"two-day lag rule" has survived the test of time. If the event is important, completely rest three days before and perhaps four days before if possible. Please don't try to add weeks, months or years of hard work and training into the last week.

8. The airline industry was made safer because of checklists. Use this simple formula for success: Make checklists and follow them. If you need them for your warmup or mobility work or whatever, make them. I'm reminded of the football team that showed up to a game without footballs—I remember this because I was the head coach. Use your lists to free up space in your brain to focus on the work at hand.

9. Evaluate any program or system every two weeks. Make small course corrections when you're still basically on target.

10. Be sure (!!!) to plan something for the successful completion of the program, season or system. Look after the finish line, so to speak. Answer "Now what?" long before you come to that point.

Easy Strength
and the Magic Secrets of Training

Most of success is just showing up.

But "keep going" is just as important.

Easy Strength is a method of teaching people to keep showing up and keep going.

The secret to high-level performance is often simply getting the work in and staying out of your own way. I've heard dozens of stories of people ruining months or even years of planning with some new thing. It might be as simple as getting a Swedish massage just before the finals of the Olympic games for an athlete who'd never had one.

"It was free!"

True. Sadly, the athlete left the performance moaning as all the tension left the body.

Even great coaches can fail this. Percy Cerutty allowed one of his athletes to do an experimental warmup before the finals of the Olympic Games. It didn't go well. Of course it didn't.

I've seen athletes try new techniques after watching an opponent do them. I used to add additional turns to my discus warmups just to get the opponents thinking about my technique.

I'm not sorry for it.

Easy Strength is the ultimate "show up" program. No one single workout makes a difference, but doing each lift five days a week accumulates over the two months.

Combining Easy Strength with appropriate training leads to superior performance outcomes. For the everyday trainer, Easy Strength allows you to focus on what is truly important for success: quality sleep and quality nutrition.

It's that easy.

Understanding Heavy

The essence of understanding Easy Strength comes down to a simple concept: understanding heavy. After 50-plus years of lifting, I understand the concept well. Others need more clarity.

People have told me to call this concept the "rate of perceived effort" or worse, percentages, but really, you tread on thin ice if you discuss percents too early.

I have gone through this before. I have this idea of sorta max, max and max max. If you lift once a month or so, you might have a sorta max number in a few lifts. Usually in the barbell lifts, it's a round number like 100 or 200 or a natural plate number like 135 or 225.

It's often a lie, by the way, as people (male) tend to inflate numbers. I always told my daughters if a boy bragged about a 200-pound bench to lean in softly and whisper, "Dear God, I'm so sorry."

A max would be what you might achieve after some serious effort. Perhaps you focus and train for several years and jump up to a lot more big plates and some big numbers. You discovered the fallacies of linear periodization and the need for variation. You probably had to use recovery tools to keep coming back to the lifts.

You know where this is heading: A max max is going to be a lifetime achievement where something is on the line. You have a story about your max max attempts and, no, you might never see those lifts again. Usually, my max max stories begin with, "To win, I needed to take…"

My problem with percentages, of course, is that if you bench 200, doing 90% for a double is pretty believable and 180 is certainly doable for two. Once you get to 300 or 400 pounds, that 270 for two or 360 for two will take some training to achieve.

If you get to a 600-pound bench to win the big meet, someone mentioning that you should be able to casually do a double with 540 might deserve a face slap.

Heavy is relative… and you know that.

I can remember my first serious training days as a chase, at first, for triple figures. I can look back in my journals and see myself struggling with 85 pounds in the bench, front squat and clean.

The next year, I struggled time and time again to bench 200. By the time I got to 300, I wondered what the big deal was two years before with 100.

Yet, benching 100 for the first time was a big deal. It was HEAVY. I probably needed more mental focus on making that lift than I did for lifts far heavier years later.

To be successful with Easy Strength, you need to understand these two things:

> *What is heavy?*

> *What is reasonable?*

Most of the people who email me about Easy Strength want percentages for the lifts. I email them back and tell them to find weights that are reasonable—heavy enough.

Yep, that's vague.

If you've deadlifted 700 pounds, two sets of five with 350 pounds is really light, but still heavy—350 for five is going to get the systems firing. If it feels too light, add weight next time. If that's still too light, add more the next workout. Find a load that's reasonable, repeatable and doable.

Each time I have done the full 40 days, I've had the odd courage to start lighter than my ego allowed. Quickly, I add load. Remember, there's only one rule in the 40-day approach:

Don't miss.

Ever.

If you miss a lift, you missed the whole idea of the program. Lifting five days a week and doing the same basic moves builds up an amazing amount of volume through the weeks. You're gently nudging your systems to strength.

Yes, it sounds easy.

It's called "Easy Strength."

Variation in Easy Strength

I've never been sure why I was able to handle the original 40-day workout without any confusion. It seemed clear enough:

"For the next 40 workouts, pick five lifts. Do them every workout. Never miss a rep, in fact, never even get close to struggling. Go as light as you need to go, and don't go over 10 reps for any of the movements in a workout. It's going to seem easy. When the weights feel light, simply add more weight."

Since beginning this over a decade and a half ago, I'm always stunned how people can screw it up. Sure, there were some lessons to be learned. But still.

First, I had serious maximum lifts. Doing a light workout, about 50% of maximum, still involved loads from 165 pounds in the incline bench to over 300 in the deadlift. My body, and this would be true for any body, was getting stimulus from these "light" loads.

I'm not sure if 50 pounds or 100 pounds would really gear the body up for accommodation. And, oddly, I'm also not sure these loads *wouldn't* make the body adapt.

Next, I always chose lifts that weren't my best movements.

I could bench, at the time, 405 pounds in the bench press in a polo shirt and khaki pants after work. My incline bench was 300 when I started my first attempt at Easy Strength.

I'd never really done thick-bar deadlifts, but had pulled 628 at 3:00 in the morning at a powerlifting meet. Doing a 265-pound deadlift, even with a thick bar, wasn't exactly crushing me.

By choosing lifts I knew but hadn't really mastered or maxed, I got a nice free learning curve. Strength, like flexibility, is neurological. Easy Strength is based, basically, on learning.

I told you it's like learning to type. You can't force people to type faster until they know where the keys are, and then lay down some synapses and systems to enable more speed and accuracy.

But don't think it ends there.

When the load begins to climb, the body realizes something is going on, and we get that marvelous and magical hormonal cascade that increases muscle mass in all its mysterious ways. If anyone tells you they know exactly how this process works, you may have someone practicing the gym rat's version of the Dunning-Kruger effect.

Here:

> *"Coined in 1999 by then-Cornell psychologists David Dunning and Justin Kruger, the eponymous Dunning-Kruger Effect is a cognitive bias whereby people who are incompetent at something are unable to recognize their own incompetence. And not only do they fail to recognize their incompetence, they're also likely to feel confident that they actually are competent."*

https://www.forbes.com/sites/markmurphy/2017/01/24/the-dunning-kruger-effect-shows-why-some-people-think-theyre-great-even-when-their-work-is-terrible/

Finally, I may simply be a genius. I like this answer best (my own Dunning-Kruger effect). Or, on a different level of full of myself, perhaps I can simply follow a program.

As every trainer and coach knows, that's rare.

With the benefit of all these years of experience, there are certain movements that work well:

Swings (as a warmup)

Vertical press

Vertical pull

Deadlift

Ab wheel roll

We have had many forum discussions about making squats work with Easy Strength, but they just don't work well. Toss in goblet squats in the warmup to maintain the positions for the 40 days of training.

Horizontal presses, like benches, are fine, but the need for spotters has taught me that for most of the people doing this—overwhelmingly home trainees—it isn't a good option. Horizontal pulls, basically rowing, seem to just beat up the back… experience tells us "no."

With load, the advice is simple: When the weights feel light, simply add more weight.

This has caused me more headaches than anything.

"What do you mean by light?"

You know, not heavy!

With my years in the weightroom, I've developed another sense when it comes to perceived exertion. My internal monitoring system seems to have a skill of saying quickly:

This is a stupid idea!!!!

For me, when 165 felt light, I went to 185. Oddly, that felt light faster than 165. Progress is nearly impossible to explain.

Adding load brings us to fractals and the work of Benoit B. Mandelbrot (I include a full article as an appendix for reference). When it comes to adding load, I follow Mandelbrot's three-part insight on variation:

> *Mild*
>
> *Wild*
>
> *No*

Mild sounds like "mild." If you want variation in the press, simply go from bench to incline to decline. That's mild.

When it comes to load, you can perhaps decide to add 10 pounds for upper body work and 20 for lower body work—the vanilla approach to training.

It has the same issues as linear periodization. If you bench 100 pounds and add 10 pounds a week, next year at this time you'll be benching in the low 600s.

And… good luck on that.

Mild has its value. It's excellent for exercise selection changes, and gives a bit of a path. There's a real chance that the improvement curve will flatten out fast.

Wild changes in exercise can be fun. Tommy Kono, the outstanding O lifter and Mr. Universe, used to focus on an upcoming Olympic lifting meet for eight weeks. After the meet, on the following Monday, he'd bodybuild with all its pumping and isolation. When an O lifting meet was within eight weeks, he flipped back to the press, snatch and clean and jerk.

It worked.

Improving high school athletes is often a matter of having them go from wrestling to the hurdles to football. (By the way, that's brilliant advice.) Playing one sport year-round doesn't seem to teach the lessons of sport very well. See Epstein's *Range* for details.

In terms of load, on the Easy Strength program, I like wild. At Utah State, when I first was a strength coach, we only had 45s and 25s. Here were the loads:

45

95

135

145 (25s only)

185

225

275

Certainly, you could play with the multiple 25s, but it was ugly.

When working with a freshman lifter, we could do certain lifts rather easily… up to a point. Then, a decision had to be made. Jumping up in the snatch from 135 to 185 was a big leap.

Yet, we thrived.

Literally, it was wild!

This big-leap idea works well with a full set of plates too. Why take a 395-pound attempt for a new personal record in a lift… toss on the additional load and get 400!

I liked light reasonable lifts on Easy Strength, and then the crazy jumps up.

It *is* wild!

The final option on variation is this: No.

That's right. If you ask if we should change exercises during the 40 days, the answer is no.

Oddly, not changing load is another option.

True!

John McKean is one of the least known, but most informative strength writers of all time. He reintroduced HeavyHands to strength people (with his own amazing additions), and was the first person I know to recommend training with bands. This classic article sums his great insight on Constant Weight Lifting:

> "These days I train almost entirely with fixed poundages, and relatively light ones at that, utilizing Dick Hartzell's Flex Bands along with the barbell, dumbbell or kettlebell to increase resistance near completion of a lift and to train acceleration. Even though it does not seem possible at this stage of life, my competitive all-round lifts are increasing steadily and faster than any time previously! And a note to some of you that may feel there are no 'new oceans to explore' simply because you can flip around the heaviest solid kettlebell, stay with your favorite piece of equipment and you'll always find new strength; if it worked for old Herman Goernor, it'll be good to you too!"
>
> *https://www.dragondoor.com/articles/on-constant-weight-training/*

Is it possible to improve just doing two sets of five with five basic lifts with the same load for 40 days? Yes, I think so. I haven't tried it yet, but my experiences have taught me that we should never ignore the simple but elegant.

There is a truth in Easy Strength: For 40 days, you're choosing to "Do this!" In a world where opinion and fashion change faster than a chameleon, this approach is like fine wine or great music.

It seems to get better over time.

Easy Strength Approach to O Lifting

If you follow my work, you know my Movement Matrix. Here's another look at it:

MOVEMENT	PLANKS AS A PROGRAM	STRENGTH TRAINING *LESS THAN 10 REPS* HYPERTROPHY *15–25 REPS*	ANTI-ROTATION WORK	TRIADS	OLYMPIC LIFTS
PUSH	**PUPPs** Plank	(Bench) Press Pushup	One-arm Bench Press One-arm Over-head Press		
PULL	**Bat Wing**	Pullup Row	One-arm TRX Row	Push Press/Jerk	Squat Snatch
HINGE	**Glute Bridge with AB Hold**	Hip Thrust Rack DLs Goad Bag Swing	**Hill Sprints Stadium Steps** Skipping Bounding High Knee Work	Swings	Clean and Jerk
SQUAT	**Goblet Squats** 6-point Rocks	Double KB Front Squat The Full Squat Family	**Bear Hug Carries** Bear Crawls Bear Hug Carries with Monster Walk	LitviSprints/LitviSleds	
LOADED CARRY	**Farmer's Walk** Horn Walk	Prowler Car Push	One-arm Carries: **Suitcase Carry** Waiter Walk Rack Walk		

On the far right, you find the two lifts in the sport of Olympic lifting. Winning in the O lifts requires that you have the highest total of those two lifts in your weight category. It's a sport, but the lifts can also be used to train other athletes.

In my world, the O lifts are foundational movements for football, throwing and everything else, IF we have the time and the appropriate mobility, flexibility and fitness.

I get lots of requests for programming the O lifts, but the issue is always multi-faceted.

   1. Do you have an Olympic bar and a place to drop weights?

   2. Do you know the lifts?

   3. What are your records in the snatch, clean and jerk, and total?

   4. Why are you asking me to help you online?

Each answer is key. With question four, I often discover the person is broken, damaged and destroyed by trying to train like a drugged up full-time lifter who sleeps, trains and eats… and who has somebody making those meals.

Often, I suggest an Easy Strength approach with appropriate poundage and percentages. This is nothing new—the casual trainer can make great progress focusing on the O lifts and ONE conditioning tool. The weight is usually in the 70–80% range, and we only go heavy on the platform at a meet with three officials.

And, yes, I wish I would have done this myself!

The Easy Strength O lift program is simply a five-day a week training plan involving three weeks of:

   Snatch

   Clean and jerk

   Farmer walks or prowlers or sled pulls (vary it as you wish)

Then, a single week of:

> *Power snatch*
>
> *Power clean*
>
> *Front squats*

That's it.

With the Olympic lift training, for a non-national or non-world-class lifter, it's going to be a study in picking options—more on this in a moment. I feel the performance of the Olympic lifts is oddly the smartest training in sports. We can include the power lifts here too.

Your sport blends the technical training with the strength (plus mobility and flexibility) training at the same time.

Adding the loaded carries and the front squats are for conditioning and work capacity purposes. Yes, if necessary, drop those! But I wouldn't recommend it.

Quickly, the rules:

- Never miss an attempt in training. If you do, you really missed the point of this whole program.

- Strive to use the "heels only" technique.

- Always finish fresh… and enthusiastic.

WEEKS ONE, TWO AND THREE

Day One (training five days a week)

> Snatch: Five sets of two with a single weight
>
> Clean and jerk: Five sets of singles with a single weight
>
> Farmer walks or prowlers or sled pulls

Day Two

> Snatch: Three sets of three with a heavier load than day one (the increase can be one kilo)

> Clean and jerk: Three singles with a heavier load than day one

> Farmer walks or prowlers or sled pulls

Day Three

> Snatch: Two sets of five with a lighter load

> Clean and jerk: Five singles with a lighter load

> Farmer walks or prowlers or sled pulls

Day Four

> Snatch: Five sets of two with a single weight

> Clean and jerk: Five sets of singles with a single weight

> Farmer walks or prowlers or sled pulls

The secret to the program: Go a little heavier than day one, but try to see if it "feels" the same.

Day Five

> Snatch: One set of five, add weight, then do a set of three, add weight for a double

> Clean and jerk: Three singles adding weight each time

> Farmer walks or prowlers or sled pulls

Measure progress by the day one and day four loads: These should nudge upward monthly.

On week three, day five: Strive for heavier and heavier attempts each month.

WEEK FOUR

Day One

Power snatch: Three sets of three

Power clean: Three sets of three

Front squat: Three sets of three

Day Two

Power snatch: Two sets of five
(fast and snappy... find a good load)

Power clean: Two sets of five
(fast and snappy... find a good load)

Front squat: Two sets of five
(fast and snappy... find a good load)

Day Three

Go heavier than day one

Power snatch: Three sets of three

Power clean: Three sets of three

Front squat: Three sets of three

Day Four

Repeat the load from day two (go heavier next month)

Power snatch: Two sets of five

Power clean: Two sets of five

Front squat: Two sets of five

Day Five

Go heavier than day three (if reasonable)

Power snatch: Three sets of three

Power clean: Three sets of three

Front squat: Three sets of three

Although I don't trust percentages for most people, an experienced lifter would think about 65–70% (or less) on the first round. Oddly, you might feel so good that you jump up really heavy and…

Miss the point of the program!

The volume is deceptive. My math skills are always suspect, but it appears we're doing 18 quality sets of snatches each week for weeks one through three, and 21 sets of basically singles in the clean and jerk.

My coach, Dave Turner, got me to understand, too late in my career, that the clean and jerk takes a high toll on the body.

Singles are fine.

Can you do more? Well, try this first.

My goal for you is to have a full month of "makes" and grease the positions and patterns. After the second full month, invent a meet, go heavy, see how you feel and how you do.

You're going to argue it's too easy.

Until you do it.

Combining the Easy Strength O Lifting with Fasting and Complexes

The Easy Strength O lifting program had been working well for a number of our test subjects. The magic of ES was working, but, as always, there's a bit of need for many of us for more.

At the same time, I'd been discussing combining fasting and quick morning workouts with Pat Flynn. The aim was for combining a 15-hour fast with a fast workout to improve health, fitness and body composition.

My life was transformed by adopting some of the methods of fasting. Certainly, it's nothing new; Hippocrates advised it for obesity, and every religious tradition utilizes it for spiritual discipline.

Along with some medical interventions—I was born with a condition called "Pistol Grip Hips" and both needed to be replaced... I was able to put it off for six decades!—fasting changed my body composition AND my relationship with food.

I quickly learned that hunger was really not that big of a deal. I found out that not eating was a choice, and a choice I needed to make each day. I also discovered by not grazing all day long, I made better meal choices... and I looked a lot better.

And, maybe, there's a bit of magic in doing a workout while fasted. Some argue this is crazy, but the results speak for themselves.

The following program is based on Pirate Map thinking. It could be summed like this:

- The day begins the night before. Make a to-do list. Relax. Practice appropriate sleep hygiene. I prepare the coffee for the following morning, and I wake up to smell of coffee.

- Wake up, take a moment to be grateful, and do not hit the snooze button.

- Extend your fast until you do session one, the Complexes.

- Eat! Live your life.

- Later in the day, do the Olympic lifting session.

- Eat! Live your life!

- Repeat!

The program calls for two workouts a day. If you try this, you'll discover both workouts add up to about 30 minutes of effort. That's not much. Most people who follow the program discover (as I did on the original) there's little need for warmups. Certainly, do what you need to do, but it might not be much.

I discovered my warmup needs became less and less until I'd just walk into the gym and go. My insight was that, and please forgive me for saying it, I was becoming a lifting machine.

I had taught myself to be ready to lift anytime and anywhere. Percy Cerutty once noted that if you pour water on a cat, it doesn't warm up or stretch out before it bounds away... or worse.

Easy Strength teaches us that our abilities are always at the ready.

As you progress on the program, see if this insight about warmups applies to you too.

The Fast-15
Easy Strength Olympic Lifting Program

The title of this program is from a discussion I had with Pat Flynn. Pat believes in having two windows of training each day. One is in a fasted state and the other would be the more traditional training system. He wants people to fast for 15 hours before the first session, hence: Fast-15. Be sure to follow the earlier Pirate Map.

WEEK ONE

Day One (training five days a week)

Prep the to-do list the night before; calm "somehow" before sleep; don't hit the snooze button in the morning.

Fast for 15 hours.

Complex A—three sets of five… all with the same light weight:

Row

Clean

Front squat

Military press

Back squat

Good mornings

Eat protein and veggies. Drink water. Add a protein drink.

Next Session

> *Snatch:* Five sets of two with a single weight
>
> *Clean and jerk:* Five sets of singles with a single weight
>
> *Farmer walks or prowlers or sled pulls*

Day Two

> Prep the to-do list the night before; calm "somehow" before sleep; don't hit the snooze button in the morning.
>
> *Fast for 15 hours.*

Complex C—it's called "C," from the work I've done in the past. This program uses "A" and "C" and doesn't use the others. Three sets of five, all with the same light weight:

> *Hang snatch*
>
> *Overhead squat*
>
> *Back squat*
>
> *Good mornings*
>
> *Row*
>
> *Deadlift*

Eat protein and veggies. Drink water. Add a protein drink.

Next Session

> *Snatch:* Three sets of three with a heavier load than day one (it can be just a kilo)
>
> *Clean and jerk:* Three singles with a heavier load than day one
>
> *Farmer walks or prowlers or sled pulls*

Day Three

Prep the to-do list the night before; calm "somehow" before sleep; don't hit the snooze button in the morning.

Fast for 15 hours.

Complex A—three sets of five... first two sets same as last time, with the last set heavier:

Row

Clean

Front squat

Military press

Back squat

Good mornings

Eat protein and veggies. Drink water. Add a protein drink.

Next Session

Snatch: Two sets of five with a lighter load

Clean and jerk: Five singles with a lighter load

Farmer walks or prowlers or sled pulls

Day Four

Prep the to-do list the night before; calm "somehow" before sleep; don't hit the snooze button in the morning.

Fast for 15 hours.

Complex C—three sets of five... first two sets same as last time, with the last set heavier:

> *Hang snatch*
>
> *Overhead squat*
>
> *Back squat*
>
> *Good mornings*
>
> *Row*
>
> *Deadlift*

Eat protein and veggies. Drink water. Add a protein drink.

Next Session

> *Snatch*: Five sets of two with a single weight
>
> *Clean and jerk*: Five sets of singles with a single weight
>
> *Farmer walks or prowlers or sled pulls*

The secret to the program: Try to go a little heavier than day one, but see if it "feels" the same.

Day Five

> Prep the to-do list the night before; calm "somehow" before sleep; don't hit the snooze button in the morning.
>
> *Fast for 15 hours.*

Complex A—Three sets of five... first set same as last time, last two sets heavier:

> *Row*
>
> *Clean*
>
> *Front squat*
>
> *Military press*
>
> *Back squat*
>
> *Good mornings*

Eat protein and veggies. Drink water. Add a protein drink.

Next Session

> *Snatch:* One set of five, add weight, a set of three, add weight for a double
>
> *Clean and jerk:* Three singles adding weight each time
>
> *Farmer walks or prowlers or sled pulls*

Measure progress by the day one and day four loads—these should nudge upward monthly.

WEEK TWO

Day One (training five days a week)

> Prep the to-do list the night before; calm "somehow" before sleep; don't hit the snooze button in the morning.
>
> *Fast for 15 hours.*

Complex C—Three sets of five… first set same as last time, last two sets heavier:

> *Hang snatch*
>
> *Overhead squat*
>
> *Back squat*
>
> *Good mornings*
>
> *Row*
>
> *Deadlift*

Eat protein and veggies. Drink water. Add a protein drink.

Next Session

> *Snatch:* Five sets of two with a single weight
>
> *Clean and jerk:* Five sets of singles with a single weight
>
> *Farmer walks or prowlers or sled pulls*

Day Two

Prep the to-do list the night before; calm "somehow" before sleep; don't hit the snooze button in the morning.

Fast for 15 hours.

Complex A—three sets of five... all three sets with the heavier weight:

Row

Clean

Front squat

Military press

Back squat

Good mornings

Eat protein and veggies. Drink water. Add a protein drink.

Next Session

S*natch:* Three sets of three with a heavier load than day one (it can be just one kilo)

Clean and jerk: Three singles with a heavier load than day one

Farmer walks or prowlers or sled pulls

Day Three

Prep the to-do list the night before; calm "somehow" before sleep; don't hit the snooze button in the morning.

Fast for 15 hours.

Complex C—three sets of five... all three sets with the heavier weight:

Hang snatch

Overhead squat

Back squat

Good mornings

Row

Deadlift

Eat protein and veggies. Drink water. Add a protein drink.

Next Session

Snatch: Two sets of five with a lighter load

Clean and jerk: Five singles with a lighter load

Farmer walks or prowlers or sled pulls

Day Four

Prep the to-do list the night before; calm "somehow" before sleep; don't hit the snooze button in the morning.

Fast for 15 hours.

Complex A—three sets of eight... all with a light weight:

Row

Clean

Front squat

Military press

Back squat

Good mornings

Eat protein and veggies. Drink water. Add a protein drink.

Next Session

> *Snatch:* Five sets of two with a single weight
>
> *Clean and jerk:* Five sets of singles with a single weight
>
> *Farmer walks or prowlers or sled pulls*

The secret to the program: Try to go a little heavier than day one, but see if it "feels" the same.

Day Five

> Prep the to-do list the night before; calm "somehow" before sleep; don't hit the snooze button in the morning.
>
> *Fast for 15 hours.*

Complex C—three sets of eight… all with a light weight:

> *Hang snatch*
>
> *Overhead squat*
>
> *Back squat*
>
> *Good mornings*
>
> *Row*
>
> *Deadlift*

Eat protein and veggies. Drink water. Add a protein drink.

Next Session

> *Snatch:* One set of five, add weight, a set of three, add weight for a double
>
> *Clean and jerk:* Three singles adding weight each time
>
> *Farmer walks or prowlers or sled pulls*

Measure progress by the day one and day four loads—these should nudge upward monthly.

WEEK THREE

Day One (training five days a week)

Prep the to-do list the night before; calm "somehow" before sleep; don't hit the snooze button in the morning.

Fast for 15 hours.

Complex A—three sets of eight... first two sets light, last set heavier:

Row

Clean

Front squat

Military press

Back squat

Good mornings

Eat protein and veggies. Drink water. Add a protein drink somewhere.

Next Session

Snatch: Five sets of two with a single weight

Clean and jerk: Five sets of singles with a single weight

Farmer walks or prowlers or sled pulls

Day Two

Prep the to-do list the night before; calm "somehow" before sleep; don't hit the snooze button in the morning.

Fast for 15 hours.

Complex C—three sets of eight… first two sets light, last set heavier:

Hang snatch

Overhead squat

Back squat

Good mornings

Row

Deadlift

Eat protein and veggies. Drink water. Add a protein drink.

Next Session

Snatch: Three sets of three with a heavier load than day one (it can be one kilo)

Clean and jerk: Three singles with a heavier load than day one

Farmer walks or prowlers or sled pulls

Day Three

Prep the "to-do list the night before; calm "somehow" before sleep; don't hit the snooze button in the morning.

Fast for 15 hours.

Complex A—three sets of eight… first set light, last two sets heavier:

Row

Clean

Front squat

Military press

Back squat

Good mornings

Eat protein and veggies. Drink water. Add a protein drink.

Next Session

> *Snatch:* Two sets of five with a lighter load
>
> *Clean and jerk:* Five singles with a lighter load
>
> *Farmer walks or prowlers or sled pulls*

Day Four

> Prep the to-do list the night before; calm "somehow" before sleep; don't hit the snooze button in the morning.
>
> *Fast for 15 hours.*

Complex C—three sets of eight... first set light, last two sets heavier:

> *Hang snatch*
>
> *Overhead squat*
>
> *Back squat*
>
> *Good mornings*
>
> *Row*
>
> *Deadlift*

Eat protein and veggies. Drink water. Add a protein drink.

Next Session

> *Snatch:* Five sets of two with a single weight
>
> *Clean and jerk:* Five sets of singles with a single weight
>
> *Farmer walks or prowlers or sled pulls*

The secret to the program: Try to go a little heavier than day one, but see if it "feels" the same.

Day Five

> Prep the to-do list the night before; calm "somehow" before sleep; don't hit the snooze button in the morning.
>
> *Fast for 15 hours.*

Complex A—three sets of eight... all sets with the heavier load:

> *Row*
>
> *Clean*
>
> *Front squat*
>
> *Military press*
>
> *Back squat*
>
> *Good mornings*

Eat protein and veggies. Drink water. Add a protein drink.

Next Session

> *Snatch:* One set of five, add weight, a set of three, add weight for a double
>
> *Clean and jerk:* Three singles adding weight each time
>
> *Farmer walks or prowlers or sled pulls*

Measure progress by the day one and day four loads—these should nudge upward monthly.

Week three, day five: Strive for heavier and heavier attempts each month.

WEEK FOUR
Day One

> Prep the to-do list the night before; calm "somehow" before sleep; don't hit the snooze button in the morning.
>
> *Fast for 15 hours.*

Complex C—three sets of eight... all sets with the heavier load:

Hang snatch

Overhead squat

Back squat

Good mornings

Row

Deadlift

Eat protein and veggies. Drink water. Add a protein drink.

Next Session

Power snatch: Three sets of three

Power clean: Three sets of three

Front squat: Three sets of three

Day Two

Prep the to-do list the night before; calm "somehow" before sleep; don't hit the snooze button in the morning.

Fast for 15 hours.

Complex A—three sets of three... same weight, but you can go heavier:

Row

Clean

Front squat

Military press

Back squat

Good mornings

Eat protein and veggies. Drink water. Add a protein drink.

Next Session

Power snatch: Two sets of five
(fast and snappy... find a good load)

Power clean: Two sets of five
(fast and snappy... find a good load)

Front squat: Two sets of five
(fast and snappy... find a good load)

Day Three

Prep the to-do list the night before; calm "somehow" before sleep; don't hit the snooze button in the morning.

Fast for 15 hours.

Complex C—Three sets of three... same weight, but you can go heavier than the eights and fives:

Hang snatch

Overhead squat

Back squat

Good mornings

Row

Deadlift

Eat protein and veggies. Drink water. Add a protein drink.

Next Session

Go heavier than day one.

Power snatch: Three sets of three

Power clean: Three sets of three

Front squat: Three sets of three

Day Four

Prep the to-do list the night before; calm "somehow" before sleep; don't hit the snooze button in the morning.

Fast for 15 hours.

Complex A (Three sets of three… same weight, but you can go heavier than the eights and fives):

Row

Clean

Front squat

Military press

Back squat

Good mornings

Eat protein and veggies. Drink water. Add a protein drink.

Next Session

Repeat load from day two (go heavier next month).

Power snatch: Two sets of five

Power clean: Two sets of five

Front squat: Two sets of five

Day Five

Prep the to-do list the night before; calm "somehow" before sleep; don't hit the snooze button in the morning.

Fast for 15 hours.

Complex C—three sets of three… go heavier on the last set:

Hang snatch

Overhead squat

Back squat

Good mornings

Row

Deadlift

Eat protein and veggies. Drink water. Add a protein drink.

Next Session

Go heavier than day three (if reasonable).

Power snatch: Three sets of three

Power clean: Three sets of three

Front squat: Three sets of three

Repeat this month.

After three months, test yourself in a meet or practice session.

The Post-Deployment Program

I work with a lot of people who get deployed into combat and come back tired, and sometimes a bit broken. When they log onto the internet, they're bombarded with ads for working harder and longer.

But what they need is some "mild." They need some mobility; they need some body composition work; they need time to put themselves back together.

With great volunteers—I have to thank George and Andrew for all the feedback and insights—I came up with a fairly simple program. It's the basics you know: push, pull, hinge, squat and loaded carries.

It's also a mix of Tim Anderson's Original Strength. And it's evolved into something that surprises literally everyone who tries it. It's easy, but it's hard. It's simple, but it works.

At the end of three months, we can hope for modest goals. Here you go:

GOALS FOR THE PROGRAM IN MONTH THREE

Squat bodyweight for 25 reps

Do four "hang for 30 seconds, then pull up"

Rack deadlift double bodyweight

Press more in the half-kneeling one-arm press

I chose these specifically for a good and manageable set of goals—
not the best possible improvement in the history of training. If
you can squat bodyweight for 25, I'm guessing you have some
strength and mobility and some muscle mass.

Hanging for 30 seconds is great for the grip, miraculously
improves shoulders and gives us that nice pop we call "the poor
man's chiropractor" in my gym. Doing a pullup after the hang is
tough. Doing that combo four times without letting go of the bar
takes some training—about three months of training.

The rack deadlift goal is a safe way to test overall body strength,
as well as a great test for the grip. Moreover, even tender backs
seem to like the nearly pure hinge of the movement.

The half-kneeling press demands that the hip flexors are
stretched, the pelvis and the rib box are in line and the shoulders
are powerful. This is my answer to that dumb question, "If you
could only do one lift, what would it be?"

Each movement is done in three consecutive parts. There's an
Original Strength movement, an easy variation of loaded carries
and then the lift. Many consider the OS a rest, but on weeks three
and four, you might need to rest after every set—or "round," as
we call these groups.

Push

    Prone neck nod

    Kettlebell waiter walk

    Lift (half-kneeling press)

Pull

    Prone "find your shoes"

    Kettlebell single side rack walk, down and back

    Lift (hanging pullup)

Hinge

Six-point nods

Kettlebell suitcase carry, down and back

Lift (rack deadlift: bar set at one inch above the knee the first time you go through the three-month program. The next time, try one inch below the knee.)

Squat

Six-point rock

Hip-flexor stretch

Lift (squat options follow)

Squat Options

Back squat the first three months no matter what

Front squat

Overhead squat

Depth (go deeper)

Pause (each rep!)

Remedial: goblet squat

Loaded Carry

Bear crawl

Cross crawl

The carry—whichever you're doing that day: farmer walks, bear hugs, juggernauts

For example, if doing three sets of eight:

Prone neck nod

Waiter walk

Press 20 kilos x 8

> *Prone neck nod*
>
> *Waiter walk*
>
> *Press 20 kilos x 8*
>
> *Prone neck nod*
>
> *Waiter walk*
>
> *Press 20 kilos x 8*

The waiter walk is 20 kilos or so… maybe 20 meters each arm. It's just to make sure everything is tying up.

REST PERIODS

Save for loaded carries, the Original Strength movements (nods, find your shoes and rocks) are the "rest periods." Allow them to calm you down. I've discovered that 30 seconds of OS is a shockingly long time to do these movements. We experimented up to two minutes for these… and we feel good.

If you can get two people to do this with you, the loaded carries triad should be done basically without stopping. The bear crawls are horrific, by the way. Just keeping going as best you can: one person cross crawls, another carries and the third does bear crawls.

Overall, rest as you need.

What's nice is you'll find you ease into conditioning with only one round on week one, two on two and so forth. Week one workouts tend to go very fast in months two and three… even with the tough squat sets.

TIM ANDERSON ORIGINAL STRENGTH MATERIAL

Thank you, Tim. Your contributions to the world of fitness are vastly underappreciated. You make a difference in this world.

Prone Neck Nods

- Lie on your belly
- Prop up on your elbows
- Leading with your eyes, look up and nod your head up
- Look down and nod your head down

Find Your Shoes

- Lie on your belly
- Prop up on your elbows
- Leading with your eyes, look left and rotate your head to the left
- Look right and rotate your head to the right
- Try to find your shoes

Six-Point Nods

- Get on your hands and knees
- Keep a tall sternum (flat gorilla back)
- Leading with your eyes, look up and nod your head up
- Look down and nod your head down

Six-Point Rocking

- Get on your hands and knees
- Keep a tall sternum (flat gorilla back)
- Keep your head up on the horizon
- Rock back and forth as far as you can without losing your tall sternum and without dropping your head

Grizzly Bear Crawl

- Crawl on your hands and feet
- Keep your head up on the horizon
- Keep a tall sternum (flat gorilla back)
- Keep your butt below your head—back level with the ground
- Move opposite limbs together

Cross Crawl

- Stand tall
- Touch your opposite elbow to your opposite knee
- Alternate back and forth between sides
- If you cannot touch elbow to knee without bending over, touch the opposite hand to thigh

Attempts

The following information, on sets and reps, will give you an idea on how the program ramps up monthly. Week one is always fairly short, but the reps in one set are very high. As we go through the month, the sets increase and reps decrease. You will be doing the moves and specific carries in each and every set. Week four will be a lot of Original Strength moves and loaded carries.

Then, we back off to one set again.

I thank Josh Hillis for this great insight for simple programming: one set in week one, two in two, three in three and four in four. So simple, but so effective.

SETS AND REPS

> **Week One**—1x25
>
> **Week Two**—2x15
>
> **Week Three**—3x8
>
> **Week Four**—4x5

LOAD RECOMMENDATIONS

Three-Day-a-Week Loads:

> Real light, a bit more, and a challenge

Press

With the press, the devil is in the details. I want you to do half-kneeling presses with:

> Left knee down, left hand press
>
> Right knee down, right hand press

This will also give the hip flexors a nice stretch and teach the pelvis to stay under the rib cage.

Remember, week one is 25 reps, so you need to start light. The example here is for a man who wanted to press the 28-kilo kettlebell.

Note: Typically, Wednesday's load becomes next Monday's load and Friday's load becomes Wednesday's. Also, notice the jumps in load are very small, like two kilos… five pounds.

AS ALWAYS, YOU HAVE TO "DO IT" ONE-ARM PRESS EXAMPLE		
MONTH ONE Week One	8	10	12
Week Two	10	12	14/16
Week Three	12	16	20
Week Four	16	20	24
MONTH TWO Week One	12	14	16
Week Two	14	16	20
Week Three	16	20	24
Week Four	20	24	28
MONTH THREE Week One	14	16	20
Week Two	16	20	24
Week Three	20	24	Max Double
Week Four	24	28	???

Pull

From some wonderful research from Hawaii and the experiences of improving some people's pullups by simply hanging, I'm recommending something very simple.

Month One: All straight-arm hangs for time

Month Two: All flexed-arm hangs for time

Month Three: Hang (straight arm) followed by single pullups… until test day

On week one, day one, establish a repeatable base of one single hang for time. Don't overdo it. Try to extend it on days two and three.

Week two, day one, try to match last day three's time in the two sets (easy day). Strive to increase this the two next days… beat that total on Monday in three sets and continue on. Ideally, on week four, day three, you'll comfortably beat your base time on week one on all four sets.

Next month, repeat with flexed-arm hang. This will be much more difficult.

Month three: Practice the test, 30-second hang, then one pullup. Try to build up to two reps that are easy.

Squat

If you weigh 135 or under, use the 135 goal; 136–165, use the 165 goal. If you're 166–185, use the 185 goal. From 186–205, use either 185 or 225. Everyone heavier just use 225.

MONTH ONE	MONDAY	WEDNESDAY	FRIDAY	SETS AND REPS	SQUAT GOAL 135
WEEK ONE	5	45	75	1 x 25	(25 Reps)
WEEK TWO	45	75	95	2 x 15	
WEEK THREE	75	95	115	3 x 8	
WEEK FOUR	95	115	135	4 x 5	
MONTH TWO					
WEEK ONE	75	95	115	1 x 25	
WEEK TWO	95	115	135	2 x 15	
WEEK THREE	115	135	115	3 x 8	
WEEK FOUR	135	115	135	4 x 5	
MONTH THREE					
WEEK ONE	95	75	135	1 x 25	
WEEK TWO	45	75	95	2 x 15	
WEEK THREE	75	95	115	3 x 8	
WEEK FOUR	95	115	135	4 x 5	

MONTH ONE	MONDAY	WEDNESDAY	FRIDAY	SETS AND REPS	SQUAT GOAL 165
WEEK ONE	35	75	105	1 x 25	(25 Reps)
WEEK TWO	75	105	125	2 x 15	
WEEK THREE	105	125	145	3 x 8	
WEEK FOUR	125	145	165	4 x 5	
MONTH TWO					
WEEK ONE	105	125	145	1 x 25	
WEEK TWO	125	145	165	2 x 15	
WEEK THREE	145	165	145	3 x 8	
WEEK FOUR	165	145	165	4 x 5	
MONTH THREE					
WEEK ONE	125	105	165	1 x 25	
WEEK TWO	75	105	125	2 x 15	
WEEK THREE	105	125	145	3 x 8	
WEEK FOUR	125	145	165	4 x 5	

Attempts

MONTH ONE	MONDAY	WEDNESDAY	FRIDAY	SETS AND REPS	SQUAT GOAL 185
WEEK ONE	55	95	125	1 x 25	(25 Reps)
WEEK TWO	95	125	145	2 x 15	
WEEK THREE	125	145	165	3 x 8	
WEEK FOUR	145	165	185	4 x 5	
MONTH TWO					
WEEK ONE	125	145	165	1 x 25	
WEEK TWO	145	165	185	2 x 15	
WEEK THREE	165	185	165	3 x 8	
WEEK FOUR	185	165	185	4 x 5	
MONTH THREE					
WEEK ONE	145	125	185	1 x 25	
WEEK TWO	95	125	145	2 x 15	
WEEK THREE	125	145	165	3 x 8	
WEEK FOUR	145	165	185	4 x 5	

MONTH ONE	MONDAY	WEDNESDAY	FRIDAY	SETS AND REPS	SQUAT GOAL 225
WEEK ONE	95	135	165	1 x 25	(25 Reps)
WEEK TWO	135	165	185	2 x 15	
WEEK THREE	165	185	205	3 x 8	
WEEK FOUR	185	205	225	4 x 5	
MONTH TWO					
WEEK ONE	165	185	205	1 x 25	
WEEK TWO	185	205	225	2 x 15	
WEEK THREE	205	225	205	3 x 8	
WEEK FOUR	225	205	225	4 x 5	
MONTH THREE					
WEEK ONE	185	165	225	1 x 25	
WEEK TWO	135	165	185	2 x 15	
WEEK THREE	165	185	205	3 x 8	
WEEK FOUR	185	205	225	4 x 5	

Rack Deadlift

Place the bar either in a rack or on boxes so the bar is one inch above knee height.

Stretch the hammies and hinge each and every lift. Finish in a vertical plank. I suggest going crazy light on the rack deadlifts each week with the single set of 25, sneaking up to bodyweight on the two sets of 15. You can certainly choose to go heavier, but I don't suggest pushing this exercise for these three months.

Yes, that's vague.

Oddly, these high-rep hinges can cause a lot of soreness and maybe even twinge the back if you have some poor technical reps. So… don't go there.

Remember to match the day two and day three loads on next week's days one and two. In month one, don't ever really push this lift.

That was excellent advice when I first put this program out. A couple of people misunderstood this and simply used the squat program numbers for the rack deadlift. In month three, in every case, they felt good one day and maxed out. Every experimenter easily pulled the double-bodyweight lift.

What do I know? It works, it's simple and it's logical. If you don't like thinking about load and just want to train, just use the squat numbers on the deadlifts.

Loaded Carries

Make up something new and different every workout and just enjoy pushing, dragging and carrying. That's all!

REPAIR YOUR HORMONAL CASCADE

One additional thing I mention during my presentations to the military—and this is important: Repair your hormonal cascade.

I'm no expert, but what follows is some very good advice I've stolen from other presenters.

- Get up at dawn and walk.

- Go to bed no more than two hours after it's dark.

- Sleep in the darkest room you can manage.

- You have to have hormones to sleep and love.

- You need people in your life!!!

- Sleep with human contact... or your dog.

SAMPLE WORKOUT
FOR MONTH TWO, WEEK TWO, DAY THREE

This is a 180-pound male using the kettlebell numbers from the chart for one-armed presses, rack deadlift and squat from the squat chart for 185 pounders.

Push

First set

    Prone neck nod

    Kettlebell waiter walk (down and back with a 20k bell)

    Lift (half-kneeling press)

        15 reps left hand (left knee down) with a 20k bell

        15 reps right hand (right knee down) with a 20k bell

Second set

    Prone neck nod

    Kettlebell waiter walk, down and back with a 20k bell

Lift (half-kneeling press)

> 15 reps left hand (left knee down) with a 20k bell

> 15 reps right hand (right knee down) with a 20k bell

Pull

First set

Prone "find your shoes"

Kettlebell single-side rack walk, down and back (20k bell)

Lift (hanging pullup)

Today, go for a limit flexed-arm hang—be sure to note the time.

Second set

Prone "find your shoes"

Kettlebell single-side rack walk, down and back (20k bell)

If you wish, do another round of flexed-arm hang and ease off far before failure.

Hinge

First set

Six-point nods

Kettlebell suitcase carry, down and back (20k bell)

Rack deadlift, 185x15 reps

Second set

Six-point nods

Kettlebell suitcase carry, down and back (20k bell)

Rack deadlift, 185x15 reps

Squat

> Six-point rock
>
> Hip flexor stretch
>
> Back squat, 185x15 reps
>
> Six-point rock
>
> Hip flexor stretch
>
> Back squat, 185x15 reps

Loaded Carry

First set, all for 30 meters

> Bear crawl
>
> Cross crawls
>
> Farmer walks with a 20k bell in each hand

Second set, all for 30 meters

> Bear crawl
>
> Cross crawls
>
> Farmer walks with a 20k bell in each hand

This looks like a lot on paper, but once you get the hang of combining Original Strength with all the additional carries—there's a LOT of carrying in the program—you'll see your work capacity swell.

And that's, well, swell.

Six Decades of Lessons in 50 Words

A little explanation: Somebody asked me to summarize the lessons I've learned in my life… and, I was told, KEEP IT SHORT!

I hope 50 words is not too imposing.

Make a difference.

Live. Love. Laugh.

Balance work, rest, play and pray (enjoy beauty and solitude).

Sleep soundly. Drink Water. Eat veggies and protein. Walk.

Wear your seatbelt. Don't smoke. Floss your teeth.

Put weights overhead. Pick weights off the floor. Carry weights.

Reread great books. Say thank you.

And, gentle reader, thank you!

Appendices

Appendix One—Packing

Appendix Two—How to be the Perfect Wedding Guest

Appendix Three—Fast Mimicking Diet Information

Appendix Four—The Southwood Workout

Appendix Five—The Southwood Program

Appendix Six—Reaching for the Five

Appendix Seven—The Fractals Article

Appendix Eight—Snapacity, from 40 Years with a Whistle

Appendix Nine—The Updated 10,000 Swing Challenge

Appendix Ten—The Original 10,000 Swing Program

Appendix One
Packing

I travel a lot. I'm on the road about 40 weekends a year and usually attain my Diamond status from Delta (125,000 miles) during the early spring. The tools and tricks I've learned from decades of coaching and competition have allowed me to travel for up to a month at a time with only one carryon bag.

One. Never more (quoth the Raven!)

If you need aspirin, I have some. Cough medicine… here you go.

Bouillon cubes, tea, coffee, towel (*The Hitchhiker's Guide to the Galaxy* makes this clear), snow hat, swimsuit or power cords?

Yep, I have all of them.

Traveling over the oceans and spending time overseas demands a bit of thought and discipline. Experience helps—you only want to forget key things once. Never is better, but I promise you the pain of omission makes the teaching permanent.

I want to share the basics. I don't have a cure for jet lag or stock in any of the companies I recommend, but I have ideas that work.

THE BIG TICKET ITEMS

The key to proper packing is the bag.

I have an expensive piece of luggage from a company called Away. Originally, I bought it because it carried a power package that can recharge phones.

Great idea.

Then the airlines made us remove them. They said these are a fire hazard and, well, better safe than sorry.

But here's why I have it: It fits in the overhead bins on regional jets. That's not a big deal until you fly on regional jets. It has four omni-directional wheels and can take a beating. It has a simple lock with a three-number code that's probably worthless if stolen… but good enough to keep some safety and soundness.

Inside the bag are… bags. I buy those mesh zippered travel bags in a variety of sizes, but I found I only use the medium and small. Medium bags are for clothes (more on that in just a moment), and the smalls each have their own jobs.

One medium bag holds my shirts. As you know, I only wear one brand of black Polo shirts that pop out wrinkle-free no matter what I do. I roll up to 10 of them and force them into a single medium bag. If there's extra room, I might shove a few rolled-up socks in there.

My socks come from Walgreens. They're anklets with magic copper that make them smell less than horrid. I buy them six at a time and they're all exactly the same. They're half the size of normal socks, and when I do the wash, I fold together couples as I pull them out of the dryer.

Socks and underwear generally get their own bag too. I used to buy expensive travel underwear I could wash in the sink. It worked, but they slowly turn into knives and spikes over time. Now, I buy SAXX brand, which are not only extremely comfortable, but hold up well over long flights. I don't feel like I need a spatula to get them off when I arrive at a hotel.

The last medium bag has my snow and sun stuff. In this bag:

- A pair of soft fleece gloves

- A beanie cap for cold weather

- A small quick-dry towel from a shopping mall

- My swim trunks that used to be my track uniform bottoms—they dry fast

- A pair of completely flat sandals

- An ancient pair of Nike checked shorts that can be used for whatever

- A poncho I bought in Ireland that folds into a tiny bag

- A light backpack that folds into a tiny bag

- My black workout shorts

There are many trips when NONE of this stuff gets used. Often, the bag isn't even opened. But, there have been days when I snorkeled in the morning and used the other gear to stay warm later. I've seen cold nights in Poland, Ireland and England where I used the cold weather gear nearly daily.

That backpack is a must.

As I look at the bag, I'm amazed how important this bag has been when I least expected it. And I'm amazed it all fits!

One small mesh bag has my recovery gear. I always travel with performance sleepwear. I know it costs more and some people really poo-poo this online, but I think it works. If anything, it keeps the bugs off my skin. I do sleep better wearing it… and, yes, it's expensive. But, according to the bag it comes in, it "wicks heat and sweat" and controls my core temperature.

The other benefit is if someone knocks on the door, I don't have to hide behind a towel.

I also make a little room in this bag for a lacrosse ball. I use it to loosen my feet and roll out any issues from the flights and travel… and the workouts.

The next small bag has my toiletries. Always bring a full-sized toothbrush, floss sticks and travel-sized toothpaste. I usually have two tubes. I go to the dentist three times a year (and so should you), and stock up there. I also always bring a fresh shaving blade and a comb that's been with me for ages.

I carry all of that in a ziploc baggie. In another baggie, I have Folger's coffee singles and a wide variety of teas. In addition, I always have bouillon cubes. If you don't feel well, a cup of hot bouillon will work wonders.

There's NEVER enough coffee in hotel rooms. Bring your own.

The last little baggie has medicine. I travel with plenty of headache and stomachache medicines. If you need them, you'll be happy you have them. I also keep any medicines I may be on at the time in this baggie, as well as my supplements. My supplements vary through time, but Metamucil fiber wafers are one you might want to think of adding.

People always chuckle when I discuss elimination on the road.

It's funny until it's you!

Flying causes a strange kind of "internal dehydration." If you know what I mean, you know what I mean. A package of these fiber bars at night can do miracles. Often, I also travel with single-serving oatmeal packets as, very often, it's easy to get oddly hungry at night in a flipped time zone ("I should be eating now, but it's time for bed?"). A quick microwaved oatmeal might be all you need until the morning.

I have one small travel bag that carries my chargers and international converters for my phone and computer. I used to just toss them in the bag, but having them in their own bag seems to help with wear and tear. I've tried lots of power converters, and have discovered that the ones you remember to bring are the best. In other words, don't lose them.

For my computer, I bought a power cord that fits English and Irish outlets. I'm there so much that I found this to be a wise decision. I have to put an adapter on it to use here in the States.

My computer has its own padded travel bag that seems to protect it a bit. Travel is tough on everything, so it's nice to have a little security on the thing that carries a LOT of material, information and entertainment.

I always have a Bret Contreras Glute Loop and a Perform Better black mini-band blended into the bottom of the suitcase that I use for for hip thrusts, clam shells and monster walks. Toss in some pushups, and you may rediscover how to train again. I usually do a workout just after I wake up. It really seems to help with jet lag. I dunno why.

I have one final bag that I hook on the handle. I keep earphones, eye masks, ear plugs, a set of really cool "cheater glasses" that fit in basically a toothbrush tube. It also holds anything else I might want when I don't want to have to open the luggage bag.

I just travel with my cell phone. I have a little case for it that holds my ID and credit cards.

Then, I only think of two things: phone and bag.

A quick hint on travelling with a cell phone: The day before, open every application you think you might need. I play chess, checkers and solitaire; I read via Kindle and listen to meditation guidance through two different apps. I learned the hard way that these will NOT work if they need an update. Iit was awful losing my ability to read on a trip to Japan.

Lesson learned: Check for updates BEFORE you go.

WHAT I DON'T BRING

Extra shoes—never more. I wear light, flat athletic shoes and have those extremely thin sandals.

Pants—I wear a "workout" brand of jeans, and that's it. Now, if there's a wedding or something, this changes.

Books—I love books. Occasionally, I bring my small-sized *The Hobbit* or *The Sword in the Stone* or a fitness book, but honestly, I just don't find that books work for me on planes anymore.

Exception: I may buy a mystery novel at Marrisa's, the local used bookstore, read it and leave it at the hotel book exchange when I depart. *007* books are GREAT reading in a plane, by the way.

Jackets or sweaters—the bulk of these items never gets less bulky. I use my wife's advice on this:

"Pack your bags. Take out half of your clothes and don't bring them. Look at your cash and double it."

I've bought sweaters, sweatshirts and jackets all over the world. I have a delightful Norway jacket and a wonderful Connaught Rugby sweatshirt. I brought these items home. Often, however, I leave these purchases with a friend to donate… or keep.

The most important thing about traveling: You.

It's an adventure. Enjoy it.

It's a learning experience. Learn from it.

Yes, they don't do things here like they do at home. Maybe here has it right.

Meet people. Talk. Listen. Take photos (on your phone—not a bulky camera). Go to events. Cheer on a local team. Go to the small art stores and bookstores. Visit the small museums. Say "yes" to the adventure.

Try the local food and drink.

Read the local papers as best you can.

I recommend a tour, at most, about once a week.

The rest of the time, live like you live there.

Appendix Two
How to be the Perfect Wedding Guest

AKA—How to make sure the bride doesn't want to murder you

My daughter, Lindsay, wrote this to me a week after her wedding. I thought it was wonderful. We discovered one of my favorite tools, Shark Habits, as being the easiest way to keep a bride happy.

Thomas has gotten in the groove of this husband thing. Yesterday, I came home to fresh roses on our dining room table. I'm still wondering what he did wrong, but he insists it's because he saw them, and thought of me. What a cutie.

We've spent the last week coming down from our wedding (stress release is a very real thing). I can finally talk about everything that happened over the course of the weekend without getting too emotional. I feel like I have a million things I can write about when it comes to wedding planning. (I mean, I've already been asked a million and a half questions by future brides.) But, honestly, the first thing I want to touch on has nothing to do with planning and everything to do with guest behavior—so, really nothing that brides have control over. HA.

Guests have a very precarious role when it comes to weddings. As a guest, you'd assume all you're supposed to do is show up, eat food, laugh at the right times and cry at others, and bring a gift.

And, for the most part, that's correct.

However, a weird thing happens to the bride and groom during a wedding—simultaneously nothing and everything matters at the same time. We enter this weird twilight zone where we have zero idea what time it is, where we're supposed to be and what we're supposed to be doing, but we are also noticing every little thing that every guest is doing—and cataloging it for later.

There's a big misconception that the bride and groom won't notice little things like guests not showing up on the day of the wedding, but trust me, they do.

And they remember.

Want to avoid the bride's shit list? Check off each of these, and you'll be scot free.

1. Stay at the resort or preferred hotel.

Now, this has two sides to it. The first side completely has to do with money and yes, I get it, it sucks. If there's a preferred hotel or the wedding is at a resort, you can bet the bride and groom have a block of rooms they're required to fill. If they don't fill them, it falls back on their pocketbook. If you can afford it, please, for the love of God, stay at the resort. Even if it's a little outside of your range, please try to find a way to stay.

I had guests who told me they were staying at an AirBnB and Ubering over because they found a room for $90 a night versus our $139 a night. I stared at her and did the Uber math—yeah, they probably saved $10 in the whole thing, but pissed off the bride in the process. Not good.

The other side of this, though, is much more fun—you get to witness EVERYTHING if you stay at the resort. If the groom gets too drunk in the afternoon at the dive bar on the property, you get to see his groomsmen carry him back to his room, panicking about how to get the groom sober again for the ceremony.

If the golf pro gets mad at the wedding party for not following golf cart rules, you're there to see the vein pop out of his head as he yells. If the mother of the bride decides to have a meltdown because she hates her hair, you bet you'll hear her shriek through the wall.

The best part of being the guest, though? You get to just sit back and enjoy your drink while all this transpires (offer to help where you can, though, and tip your bartender!).

2. Show up EARLY!

We were walking away from the ceremony as husband and wife and spied people still walking into our venue! Granted, our entire ceremony was only 11 minutes long, but that means those guests were 15 minutes late. Assume weddings will ALWAYS start on time. Show up at least 30 minutes early, say "hi" to other guests and take your appropriate seat 10 minutes before the magic is set to start.

3. RSVP. Seriously, RSVP. Right when you get the invitation. And a "maybe" is a NO.

My dad preaches "shark habits." Basically, it's if you have a small task on your list, get it done and out of the way right away. RSVPing to a wedding should be one of these shark habits. Seriously, just do it right when you receive it. Mark the paper and send it straight back or get online and RSVP. With the amount of communication we have these days, you should know WELL before that invitation is in your hand if you'll be attending.

We had our date set 18 months in advance, were asking for addresses 11 months in advance and had "save the date" cards on the fridge 9 months in advance. If you still don't know once that invitation is in hand, put a reminder in your calendar for a couple days before the RSVP deadline. At that point, if you're a maybe, you're a no.

We had one guest (who was a PAIN for most of the wedding) who had six in her party—she RSVPed "yes" for two and "maybe" for four. Oh, and she didn't RSVP on our website; I had to hunt her down and that was her response. The one "yes" later became a "no" because they didn't look at flights until two weeks before… which leads me to my next point…

4. If your plans change, tell the BRIDE or GROOM (unless it's the day of).

It's sad, but life happens. If your plans change and you can longer attend the wedding, tell the BRIDE or GROOM. Do NOT tell the mother or the best friend or the uncle. Step up and tell them directly. They are the ONLY people in charge of the final numbers. If possible, tell them BEFORE the final numbers are due, which is usually 72 hours before the event. Make sure it's a viable excuse—you're going to lose their respect otherwise.

If it's the day of, yes, please text the next closest person you have contact with. They will choose the best way to tell the bride or groom, if they tell them at all.

5. Bring cash!

This is seemingly simple advice, but forgotten by most people. Most brides are told that it's a bad move not to have an open bar, but bar tabs quickly add up and it's usually the first thing to get cut due to budgets.

Bring $50 in cash, and if there's an open bar, drop $20 for the bartender. If it's a cash bar, you and your date are now good to have three or so drinks each and thoroughly enjoy the dance floor.

6. Speaking of dates…

You don't get a plus one.

Let me say that again: You do not get a plus one.

One more time for the people in the back—YOU DO NOT GET A PLUS ONE.

Unless your invitation says specifically, "Lindsay AND Thomas Robinson," or "Lindsay Robinson and GUEST," you do NOT get a plus one. Do not ask the bride if you get a plus one.

Also, if the SPECIFIC person named on the invitation is unable to come, do NOT assume you're able to replace the person with someone else. In that situation, yes, feel free to ask the bride, but that's the only acceptable time to ask about plus ones.

7. Stay out of the photographer's and videographer's way.

I get it—you're excited and want to take pictures of this amazing moment of two becoming one. It's emotional. It's sweet. It's a rare moment you want to capture…

But seriously, we paid a lot of money for someone to do that with a MUCH better camera. Like a LOT of money and a much, much better camera.

The day of the wedding, the photographer and wedding coordinator have more power than the bride. Respect what they say, and please do NOT get in their way.

I may have lost my mind on my grandmother who kept stepping in front of our photographer during group photos to get a picture with her iPhone. She was asked several times to move before I finally screamed, "GRANDMA, GET THE HELL OUT OF THE WAY! WE'RE LITERALLY PAYING HER TO DO THIS FOR YOU!"

Not my shiniest moment of the wedding…

Honestly, I'd suggest just putting the camera away. Enjoy the day and pull back out during the reception to grab some fun candid photos. If you HAVE to take a picture during the ceremony or group pictures because, you know, someone is holding a gun to your head or something, take a quick glance around to make sure the photographer won't be comprised by you taking a picture.

8. The day of, don't depend on the bride and groom to know anything or be responsible for anything.

This is a weird one, I know. You'd think the bride and groom would be totally aware of everything going on at their wedding. But, trust me, they're not. They might not even remember what day it is, even after staring at the date for 18 months.

During our first look, Thomas told me he cried in the shower for 20 minutes, to which I responded, "Hey, me too!" The bride and groom experience the most intense roller coaster of emotions that just can't be explained, and even simple things like remembering when their hair appointment is easily fall out of their heads.

That being said, don't text either party about wedding details or hand them gifts if you happen to see them wandering around. I feel like this is common sense, but both of these things happened to us on the day of our wedding, so it needs to be said.

Instead you should…

9. Ask and listen to the bridal party.

The bridal party ranks in the command line after the photographer and the wedding coordinator. They've spent all day with the bride and groom and will know the answers to your questions.

Where's the bathroom? Where's the gift table? Where are we going after the wedding?

Find someone with a lot of makeup who matches someone else with a lot of makeup.

On the flip side, if the bridal party tells you to do something, DO IT. That's a direct command from the BRIDE HERSELF. We had someone completely disregard my bridesmaids' request to stay away from our first look and now she's in the back of EVERY picture. Post-wedding bridezilla came out hard when I saw those.

10. Enjoy yourself. Keep your opinions away from the bride.

The same PAIN I mentioned earlier stormed up to me during our group photos screaming, "I don't know why you even hired a photographer—I got the best picture of the night!" And then proceeds to show me this terrible photo of us at the altar. I'm sure she was trying to be funny, but… no.

If you hated the color of the bridesmaids' dresses, great. If you would have done the ceremony differently, awesome. You're totally entitled to those opinions, but do NOT tell them to the bride. She spent a lot of time picking out specific colors and planning the day down to the minute. You telling her she screwed up on a specific piece is one way to make sure she never talks to you again. Instead, take those opinions to heart and apply them to your own wedding. Hell, there's a reason we didn't do our own vows!

I feel like a total bridezilla writing this. I promise, I wasn't! In fact, 95% of our guests were absolute gems, and our wedding went off without a hitch. We for sure had the "too drunk" table and the weird family dynamics, but overall, it was the most perfect day (I know that sounds cliché, but it totally was). I wanted to write this as a therapy piece, and also for that next generation of guests who are starting to attend their first weddings.

Every wedding is different, but being an excellent guest doesn't change!

Appendix Three
Fast Mimicking Diet Information

My friend, Rick Stevens, sent me Valter Longo's book, *The Longevity Diet*. Longo's TED Talk is very good. I'm a fan of fasting for all kinds of reasons. Fasting not only has interesting health benefits, but it's also a simple way to teach the mind that hunger is just not that big a deal.

I wish I knew that lesson as a thrower!

I've done the prepacked plan twice, but it's just as easy to do it yourself. Basically, most of the days are this:

> *400 calories from veggies*
>
> *400 calories from healthy fats (nuts, olive oil)*
>
> *One multivitamin and mineral supplement*
>
> *Fish oil supplement*
>
> *Sugarless tea*
>
> *Unlimited water*

My mom argued that veggies were the answer to obesity—what got you there was starches and sugars. Honestly, we had a soup recipe as a kid that was delicious, and I found something like it if you want to give it a try.

https://www.workingmother.com/momlife/13527488/weight-watchers-minestrone-soup-recipe/

MINESTRONE SOUP

Ingredients:

Cooking spray

1 large onion, chopped

2 celery stalks, chopped

1½ medium carrots, peeled and chopped

8 ounces rutabaga, chopped

2 cubes vegetable bouillon dissolved in 3½ cups of hot water

1 14-ounce can chopped tomatoes

2 teaspoons oregano

1 ounce whole-wheat pasta shells

A dash kosher salt

A dash black pepper

Directions:

1. Coat a large saucepan with cooking spray and place on medium-high heat.

2. To the saucepan, add onion, celery, carrots and rutabaga and cook, stirring as needed, for three minutes.

3. Add vegetable broth, canned tomatoes and oregano. Bring to a boil, then turn heat to low and cook for 15 minutes.

4. Add pasta and cook for another 10 minutes.

5. Add salt and pepper to taste.

6. Serve immediately, or store in an air-tight container in the refrigerator.

According to the Weight Watchers website, this recipe has only one point. As a veggie-heavy dish, this shouldn't come as too much of a surprise.

On the new SmartPoints plan, fruits and veggies have no points. This new system is designed to "encourage you to eat more of these low-calorie, nutrient-dense, filling foods."

With some fish oil capsules and herbal tea, most of us could make this fast work easily (with the soup at meals).

As for the nuts, that works out easily too. The article where this quote came from made a lot of sense:

"According to the United States Department of Agriculture and the Pistachio Health Organization, a standard one-ounce serving of pistachios is equivalent to 49 kernels and 158 calories. This means a reduced serving of 100 calories is equivalent to about 30 pistachio kernels. An equivalent 100-calorie snack might be 10 almonds, cashews or walnuts or 16 peanuts."

https://www.livestrong.com/article/312503-how-many-pistachios-make-100-calories/

And, if you decide to eat the olives, you might discover, as I did, that they are not as "bad" as I thought:

"Olives alone have only four to five calories each. 'Low-calorie' foods contain 40 calories or less per serving, according to U.S. Food and Drug Administration labeling guidelines, and a serving of 10 green or black olives has only 40 calories. Removing the pits and stuffing them with other types of foods, such as garlic, peppers, or cheese can significantly increase the calorie content. Also, adding oil to olives as a dressing will increase the number of calories."

https://www.livestrong.com/article/296457-how-many-calories-does-an-olive-have/

I'm not telling you to do this or recommending it, but, as you may know, I never advise without doing something myself first.

I was at a workshop years ago and a guy (at the time famous) asked me about the Velocity Diet. Before I could answer, he said: "It's stupid."

I asked him if he had tried it: "No." He then said something like it's simply a "protein-sparing moderated loading fasting something… "

Ah, have you done those?

No.

Yet, you're an expert!

One of the things I try to do is get my hands dirty, then leap into the fray. Sometimes I learn a lot and sometimes I waste my time, treasure and talents.

I've had emails asking me for more information than this about the Fast Mimicking Diet. You can certainly buy the book, *The Longevity Diet,* as I did, or email me for more things I can google for you. (That was a joke).

Appendix Four
The Southwood Workout

I've been teaching since 1979. Many of my teaching colleagues were former students, and I'm amazed at the number of students I've had whom I'd also taught their parents. Yet, as old as that makes me, as many of you know, I still train like I'm 20. Or at least I think I do. I still leap into fires with things like the Velocity Diet and slosh pipes.

One time, the loudspeaker came on toward the end of my all-female weightlifting class. "Teachers, go into lockdown immediately. This is not a drill." If you've lived on another planet for the last 30 years, you might not know what this means. But every student and teacher knew what was going on—*we had an armed intruder.*

We sat in total silence for an hour, hiding from windows and doors. In my mind, I thought of my children, my godchildren, and the friends and family who were also hiding throughout the building.

It turned out the gun was only a lifelike Airsoft pellet gun. The parents of the kid later argued in the media that the school had "over-reacted." A few days later, in Finland, the story was tragically different and many students were killed.

Over-reaction? I think not.

My daughter, Kelly, later told me the kids had been discussing which room would've been the best to wait it all out in. Students were sobbing throughout the hour and many kids melted down, almost in turns. Well, nobody cried in the weightroom. Certainly, my physical size helped, but I argue there was also something else: I train warriors in the weightroom.

The girls had just finished one of the best workouts I know: The Southwood Program. Those girls had been transformed by this training program. Let me share with you the Southwood workout and, later, its cousin, the Big Five: Five by Five. Yes, I've written about the Southwood program before, but it's worth repeating.

Every so often, I get an email from a high school coach about teaching a group of kids to lift weights. The notes often sound like the task of getting kids to lift is insurmountable. Some of the coaches sound like they need a miracle worker to come in and exorcize the student body before they begin to exercise.

I always argue to these fine men and women that it can be done... easily and inexpensively. I can't claim any credit for the following program, and I'm indebted to Mr. Dave Freeman, my ninth-grade physical education coach, for making us do this!

After eight years at St. Veronica's School, I transferred to Southwood Junior High. It was a helluva transition. From Irish nuns to public school is big enough, but I was also going to play football. At 118 pounds of pure nothing, it was obvious to everyone that I needed to lift weights.

It was at this time I was introduced to Southwood's lifting program. In a portable building, the school had outlaid about 15 of those cement-filled weightlifting sets that everyone from my generation remembers as their first bar.

Mr. Freeman spent little time explaining the "rep-set" system of 8–6–4 because everybody except me knew what to do. That's part of the brilliance of the program. You learn it once and then you lift. Not exactly rocket science, but who needs rocket science on the football field?

The program was very simple. First, groups of four boys were given a bar. The bars ranged from very light, maybe 25 pounds, up to nearly a hundred pounds. Each cohort of boys would lift one at a time, put the bar down, and the next boy would lift. The four would constantly move from lifter to watcher—the bar never stopped.

The three sets wouldn't take very long. In fact, sometimes it was hard to catch your breath in time for your next set.

The reps were very simple:

> *First set: Eight repetitions*
>
> *Second set: Six repetitions*
>
> *Third set: Four repetitions*

The goal was also clear-cut: When you got all 18 reps, add weight. If you started with a bar that was too light, you'd be bumped up to the next weight and a stronger group in the next workout. Of course, actual variations could include making an entirely new group with more weight too—whatever was necessary to help the group work together.

The program involved four lifts:

> *Power clean*
>
> *Military press*
>
> *Front squat*
>
> *Bench press*

Each lift was done in the 8–6–4-rep format. The bar was cleaned (once) for the set of military presses, and the bar was also cleaned (once) for the front squats. Each workout, the athlete cleaned the bar from the ground to the chest 22 times. If, as some people believe, the power clean is the "king of the exercises," that's a lot of reps with the king!

To hurry up the training (as if necessary), there were times when Mr. Freeman recommended combining the power clean and military presses. One clean and one press, repeated for a total of eight reps. This was done with a lighter weight. One could also do the front squats after the clean and presses. I've only done this once, and it was an amazing cardiovascular workout.

Each day to warm up, we had to run two laps and complete an obstacle course. The two laps were about 600 meters. The obstacle course had a wall, various upper body challenges and some balance walking.

All in all, this isn't a bad program.

Appendix Five
The Southwood Program

Now for some details on the Southwood Program, which is to be performed three days a week in the weightroom:

Power clean: 8–6–4 reps

Military press: 8–6–4 reps

Front squat: 8–6–4 reps

Bench press: 8–6–4 reps

As I began coaching, I adapted this workout several times. One thing I've returned to with training groups is to no longer use the racks on the bench press. Instead, the two spotters deadlift the weight, and bring it over the head of the athlete.

I discovered that young athletes don't set their shoulders right when they get a lift off, but naturally grab the barbell correctly when two spotters raise the bar over their eyes. Also, this method ensures proper spotting because you simply don't have time to start doing something stupid.

There are three basic methods for doing the Southwood workout. The first, or the "classic" as we call it, is to use one bar with one weight for all four exercises. The military press is what holds the athlete back on this variation.

The upside of this variation—and this is something to think about—is that the athletes aren't afraid to go deep with the lighter weight in the front squat. Since depth is more important than weight in the early learning process, this classic variation might be the best.

However, the kids really know they can do much more in the bench press. I usually find them doing lots of extra sets on their own after the formal workout ends. But… I don't see the issue of athletes doing extra work on their own as a real problem.

The second option is to change the weights for each exercise. The front squat will still be held back by the power clean, but an athlete who's early in the learning curve can get by with less weight on the front squat.

I'm a firm believer in movement over muscles, and I believe more in correct movement over weight. In other words, I don't think a 600-pound front squat is a "quad exercise," as you better have your whole body ready for the hit. And, if you barely bend your knees, don't brag about your big squat either.

In a large group setting, this requires a lot of plate changing and juggling of athletes here and there. But this second variation is great for a group up to about 20, as well as being ideal for individual athletes.

The final variation I use is simply to use the Southwood workout as a warmup.

Now, I know everybody in the world is advanced by now, but there's something about doing four big movements to get the body going. As with Alwyn Cosgrove's complexes, there's some fat burning in all of this whole-body lifting.

For fun, try doing the eight power cleans, military presses and front squats back-to-back-to-back. Continue with the six reps and finish by tackling the four-rep sets.

I tried doing the bench presses in this cluster, but found I was wrestling with the bar too much getting up and down. Certainly, safety is a concern, but I found it just too taxing for a warmup.

Appendix Six
Reaching for the Five

From the Southwood Program, we progress to the Big Five Workout. It's a simple linear progression using five sets of five reps of the same four lifts, with deadlifts added to the mix.

With this, athletes simply add weight each set so they finish the fifth set as heavy as they can go. With young male and female athletes at any level, you might find they can lift within 10 pounds of their max single for five reps. This doesn't happen to lifters with more than two or three years in the gym, but for a young lifter, this isn't uncommon.

The next workout looks like this:

> *Power clean: 5x5*
>
> *Military press: 5x5*
>
> *Front squat: 5x5*
>
> *Bench press: 5x5*
>
> *Deadlift (any variation): 5x5*

This Big Five workout is one anyone would recognize from the annals of bodybuilding history. The late Reg Park used this with great success and his devotee, an Austrian bodybuilder with political ambitions, followed a very similar program.

THE 5–3–2 WORKOUT

Every fifth workout, we change one small thing by playing with the reps and sets. Here we shift to just three sets. A set of five, add weight, a set of three, add weight, and then a heavy double. This is the 5–3–2 workout. The goal is to go as heavy as possible on the double.

The problem with going heavy on singles with young athletes is we run into that old phrase, "fuzzy logic." It's one of those phrases that got beat to death a decade ago, and seems to have fallen into the same bin as "have a cow, man" and "I didn't inhale."

When most people go heavy on singles, the spotters help "a little" and the depth gets suspect on squats. The legs work harder on military presses, and the list goes on. With a double, we can always be assured at least one repetition was really a rep.

We don't want fuzzy maxes in the weight room.

The reason I moved to every fifth session 5–3–2 workout is simple: I started to see the athletes really improve as the volume of the five by fives built up. An easier test day every two weeks seems to keep the athletes' enthusiasm high and keeps them coming back for more.

I don't worry about boring athletes when they're making progress. There's nothing worse than a program that's both boring and non-progressive. Sadly, "boring and non-progressive" defines most training programs.

After three, or at most, four weeks of the Southwood program, I shift to the Big Five. After two months of work on the Big Five with the chance of maxing four times during the two months, and with a final max day at the end, the athletes now move onto other programs.

MASTERING THE MAJOR FIVE

There's a level of mastery in the five major lifts that's evident to the eye of any visitor. There's also a lot of weight on some of the bars as sophomores sneak into the 200s on power cleans for a set of five. That's some good lifting for an adult, and amazing from a 15-year-old.

The Southwood and the Big Five are just two of the many things I've used to indoctrinate students into the world of lifting, fitness and health. I've had many students really buy into the program. They've supplemented their diets with fish oil capsules multiple times a day, and tossed back a protein shake before, halfway through and at the end of their workouts. The gains in hypertrophy and strength are impressive.

After a few weeks of doing battle with the weights, these students are ready for anything.

Appendix Seven
The Fractals Article

The autobiography, *The Fractalist: Memoir of a Scientific Maverick*, finished after the scientist's death, is a rare insight into the mind of Benoit B. Mandelbrot. Obviously, the man was born with an extraordinary mind, but circumstances… and well-timed advice… allowed him to dip his toes into the waters of many different disciplines.

Because he was able to talk and read and discuss materials from areas across the academic spectrum (dam building and telephone issues basically at once), he was able to see patterns emerge.

I base much of my coaching on his work, and I don't think I realized this. We've all been stealing Pareto's Law (Paredo)—the 80/20 Rule—since… whenever it became a cliché in the fitness business. The 80/20 rule has now morphed more into the worlds of minimalism and bio-hacking, but the basic truths are certainly evident in coaching.

Talking with Pat Flynn recently, we were, as we often do, discussing the particular issues with early specialization. David Epstein's book, *Range*, dismantles the notion of 10,000 hours of practice except in areas that have instant feedback like:

Golf

Chess

Classical music

Parents who push their kids there can "win." Sadly, of course, early specialization leads to mental and emotional burnout and lifelong issues with injuries in many sports. Specialization is fine for fish, but humans seem to need to fit in any and all environments.

Pat is a fan of generalism, the idea that learning something from, for example, the guitar, might help you in your interests in another area. Certainly, we find young athletes who play multiple sports transfer skills and tactics from this to that. One of my MLB guys told me his youth spent doing gymnastics and BMX racing did far more for him long-term than his friends who spent all their time on the diamond.

Successful athletes often note that soccer made them better at basketball... or whatever. As a coach, I always found that kids who wrestled and competed in track and field arrived to football practice with a set of skills we simply couldn't teach.

Pareto's Law leads down this popular path to minimalism.

Off eBay, I bought the first workout booklet I'd ever seen written by baseball legend Ted Williams. In it, he basically recommends:

- Put weights overhead

- Pick weights off the floor

- Focus on two sets of five

I read this in 1965 and it remains true today.

In 2002, I added:

- Carry weights for time or distance

But Williams' point is still valid.

There are many minimalist training programs that are simply:

Press

Deadlift (or kettlebell swing or snatch)

I just saved you a lot of money in books!

Fractals are, sadly, now tougher for me to define.

Mandelbrot said this:

"Clouds are not spheres, mountains are not cones, coastlines are not circles, and bark is not smooth, nor does lightning travel in a straight line."

Thankfully, I have always been helped by *Jurassic Park* defining this concept of the fractal:

"And that's how things are. A day is like a whole life. You start out doing one thing, but end up doing something else, plan to run an errand, but never get there... And at the end of your life, your whole existence has the same haphazard quality too. Your whole life has the same shape as a single day."
~ Michael Crichton, Jurassic Park

This is how I use the concept: I use the athletic career as the model for planning the year, the week and the day. We want to end on a high note, so we finish practice with a bang.

"Last throw, best throw!"

With normal people—the general population—I try to have the difficult part of the workout (like middle age!) in the middle of the training session. We begin the day by rolling around like babies and finish with a quiet breathing drill at the end of our workout in a position known in yoga as the corpse pose. We begin like babies, stand up and get back down, train hard, then slowly ease off. It's like life.

Mandelbrot also provides us with an insight about planning changes with athletes and everybody else:

Mild

Wild

Mild is the standard of "little and often over the long haul." It's how you save for retirement and how you learn to read and do math. It's also a great way to stay in shape, diet and prepare for most things in life.

Changes in a training program, especially exercise selection, are usually best described as, "Same, but different." Change the angle, change the piece of equipment, or change body position (like, from standing to half-kneeling)—that's all we usually need to do. Add a little load and continue down this path.

It works. You will be fine.

That's "mild."

Mild works.

Sometimes, however, there's a need for big, sweeping changes.

This is the time for wild!

Most of the time I train people, the workouts are basic and repeatable. Most of the time, the diet is fairly tame: protein, veggies, water and whatever else fills the plate.

But, the body—and it seems all of nature—likes an occasional shakeup.

This is the time for those two-to-six-week programs and diets I call "Bus Bench:" We're EXPECTING a change.

It's time to go wild.

Years ago—I know you know this—I did the Velocity Diet, six protein shakes a day… and that's it. It completely changed my vision as an athlete. Oh, and yes, it was REALLY hard!

Getting my throwers ready for track season, we do the three-week Big 21, and by week three, their sleep is disrupted by the fear of the next session.

The key is "after:" After the workouts… after the diet.

The athlete is rewired physically, emotionally and mentally *after* these programs.

After the disasters, nature returns much faster than anyone expects. After the wild diets and training programs, the athletes (and also normal people) rebound much quicker than they can imagine while dreaming about desserts and painless walking.

Reading Mandelbrot's book changed my understanding about how I coach and compete. I understand much better why some things worked and why other great ideas failed miserably.

"Mild" and "wild" approaches both have value. Most of the time, stay mild.

And sometimes—not often—go wild.

Appendix Eight
Snapacity, from 40 Years with a Whistle

Since the book *Arnold: The Education of a Bodybuilder* was published, most people have the mental picture that when we say "weightlifting," the audience hears "bodybuilding." Certainly, the lifting toolkit can do wonders for lean body mass, especially for hypertrophy.

But, we can go too far here: When training athletes and people from collision occupations, we must remember that performance is the key. My worst-selling book, *Now What?*, will continue to do poorly because I tell people that health is the optimal interplay of the human organs, fitness is doing a task, longevity is both quality and quantity, and performance is when they call your name and you do something.

I didn't mention ripped abs and barn-door delts. My mistake.

For performance, you need something else. Since I couldn't find a word to describe it, I invented my own (something I tend to do more and more as I age): Snapacity—pronounced snap ASS city. It's this:

Snapacity is combining explosive effort (snap) with work capacity training. You see… snapacity.

The road to attaining snapacity obviously involves intelligent training design and time. It involves the weightroom and training field. But, before we get into the specifics, we need to review something many people miss when it comes to training:

What EXACTLY are we trying to build in the weightroom?

I explain this, in my usual adolescent idiocy, with the concept, "Pull my finger?" Don't worry, you're safe; this is just a way to explain the role of strength training. The role of strength training for the athlete and collision occupation person comes down to the three Ps:

> *Point*
>
> *Push*
>
> *snaP*

This is a very simple explanation, but follow along please. Point your index finger. Now, gently, with the other hand, tug and pull the finger… but resist the tugs and pulls.

Obviously, this is planking. I'm a great believer in planking, as it teaches the most overlooked concept in correct training: tension.

Teaching people tension is the foundation of strength training. It's far more than just popping on the ground and holding a pushup-position plank (PUPP) for a few minutes. To lift massive loads, one must learn to lock down the body, armor up and resist gravity.

In 1970, I walked over to the Orange Library in South San Francisco and looked on the shelves for books on football and books on getting bigger. This single adventure led me to *The Sword in the Stone, Seven Days to Sunday* and Myles Callum's book, *Body-building and Self-defense.*

These three books, without question, changed my life. At the time, Callum's book was the most important. The other two books will have their own stories for another time.

Not long ago, I found the book online and bought it again. In this book, published in 1962, I found the following illuminating:

"This method (isometrics/tension) is based on a new theory of muscle growth. German and American scientists and doctors have found that a muscle can grow at only a certain rate. And, according to this theory, it doesn't take as much work as we used to think. If you flex any muscle to its maximum power and contraction, and hold it there for six seconds, once a day, the scientists say, the muscle will grow in strength just as fast as it can grow. (*in strength!!!*)

"Whether or not this method of muscle tension can ever really replace weight-lifting is still a matter of controversy. Some scientists say it can; endless repeating of strenuous exercise, they say, 'does not make the strength of a muscle grow any faster.' Weight-lifting, however, may make the size of the muscle grow faster."

The italics—*in strength!*—is my little helpful hint. You see, I read this book in 1970, but I continue to relearn this part:

"Some scientists say it can; endless repeating of strenuous exercise, they say, 'does not make the strength of a muscle grow any faster.' Weight-lifting, however, may make the size of the muscle grow faster."

Isometrics and the whole family of planks teach tension. In our "pull my finger" model, these teach "point." But, you can see that tension/planking/pointing are leading directly to our next P:

Push

I learned typing in 1971. I'm a far better typist today than when I pounded the keys on a manual typewriter at Southwood Junior High School. The reason we get better and better at typing is the same reason repetitions are so important in lifting... and practically everything else: Repetition teaches the nervous system. When I type, I 'P'ush my fingers to strike the keys, and the magic happens.

All too often, that's where most trainers in the weightroom begin and end. Here you go: five sets of five in various exercises on machines, and thank you for very much for showing up today. What makes the push so important in the three Ps of performance is also the reason most of us fall in love with it.

Lifting weights with appropriate movements, appropriate sets, appropriate repetitions and appropriate load set the body up for that wonderful hormonal cascade Robb Wolf explained to me years ago.

When I first learned to actually lift, my bodyweight rose from 162 pounds to 202 pounds in four months. The calories in/calories out model can't explain that kind of growth. All those front squats and O lifts with Dick Notmeyer told my body something simple: Grow or die!

I grew.

The final piece of the three Ps is snaP. Pointing your finger can give directions, pushing your finger can type words on a screen, but to make sound, you snaP your fingers.

Snapping the fingers relies on tension, timing and release. If you use too much tension, nothing happens. If you use too little, it won't make a sound. If you do it right, your snap can be heard across an auditorium.

Throwing, striking and kicking are ways to see this snaP in the real world. I believe it should be part of everyone's training.

Each of the three Ps MUST be part of an organized program. There are times for individual work on each, but the best approach is to weave them all together.

I have been working on my weightlifting matrix probably since 1970 after reading Callum's book. I have little drawings in my old journals of me attempting to do a full body workout and I put little Xs on the parts I trained. I now believe the body is one piece, but I can understand what I was trying to do.

MOVEMENT	PLANKS AS A PROGRAM	STRENGTH TRAINING *LESS THAN 10 REPS* HYPERTROPHY *15–25 REPS*	ANTI-ROTATION WORK	TRIADS	OLYMPIC LIFTS
PUSH	PUPPs Plank	(Bench) Press Pushup	One-arm Bench Press One-arm Over-head Press		
PULL	Bat Wing	Pullup Row	One-arm TRX Row	Push Press/Jerk　Swings　LitviSprints/LitviSleds	Squat Snatch　Clean and Jerk
HINGE	Glute Bridge with AB Hold	Hip Thrust Rack DLs Goad Bag Swing	**Hill Sprints** **Stadium Steps** Skipping Bounding High Knee Work		
SQUAT	Goblet Squats 6-point Rocks	Double KB Front Squat The Full Squat Family	**Bear Hug** **Carries** Bear Crawls Bear Hug Carries with Monster Walk		
LOADED CARRY	Farmer's Walk Horn Walk	Prowler Car Push	One-arm Carries: **Suitcase Carry** Waiter Walk Rack Walk		

There are 37 movements listed, and most people quickly learn almost all of them. I see them as progressive. *Progressive Resistance Exercise*, the title of Thomas DeLorme's book that gave us the basic standards of weight training language, needs to be, ummm, progressive.

But, progressive doesn't just mean MORE WEIGHT!!!

- *From isometric to ballistic (no movement to fast movement)*

- *Single movements to compound movements*

- *Equipment choices progress (or regress, if you're old school and only love iron)*

- *Exercise selection logically evolves (builds upon success)*

- *Reps and sets progress (or reduce, if using a lot of load)*

- *And, then, yes: load*

To Olympic lift—the movements on the right of the matrix—one needs to be able to flow through the Three Ps in a harmonic flow. To jerk, for example, you need to really stay tight, dip, snap, catch the weight and recover. It's a snapping plank! Or, a planking snap!

One quick point about the Matrix: the **bold** printed words are basically no (or minimal) equipment movements:

PUPP

Bat wing

Gluteal bridge/hip thrust

Goblet squat

Farmer's walk/horn walk

Hill sprints

Stadium steps

Bear-hug carries

Suitcase carries

For bear-hug carries, I often have military or American football players just pick up a teammate (bear HUG!) and walk away. Yes, it can be that simple.

Let's look at the Matrix a bit closer.

On the far-left column, I labeled it "Planks as a Program." There's great value in an annual revisiting of this list. The push, pull and hinge movements are measured by good old time under tension. It helps to have a trainer ensure that you're not just holding the position, but truly tensing everything in the body.

I tell my groups that both the goblet squat and farmer walk are moving planks. My first published article in the field of fitness was about the overhead squat. It took me years to realize the reason this movement helped throwers so much was the moving plank-ness of the lift.

Yes, it calls for mobility, flexibility, squat ability and pure strength, but it also keeps changing these qualities every inch of the way down and up.

Use "Planks as a Program" mixed with Tim Anderson's Original Strength as shown on the following page. His resets not only provide a fair amount of mobility and vestibular work, but they also get the person to ease off the tension—to relax.

I have yet to find a simpler method than Tim's for getting people back to where they should be.

MOVEMENT	PLANKS AS A PROGRAM	ORIGINAL STRENGTH PERFORMANCE RESETS
PUSH	**PUPPs** Plank	Prone Neck Work Bird Dog Family
PULL	**Bat Wing**	Prone Neck Work Elbow Rolls
HINGE	**Glute Bridge with AB Hold**	Six-Point Nods and Rocks Bird Dog Family
SQUAT	**Goblet Squats** 6-point Rocks	Prone Neck Work Hip Flexor Stretch/Rolling
LOADED CARRY	**Farmer's Walk** Horn Walk	Crawling and Cross Crawls

The next column is what most of us know: the traditional strength and bodybuilding moves. I have a few suggestions for "most of the time:"

- The total number of reps for the push, pull and squat should always be the same amount (most people do FAR too many pushes!).

- For strength, keep the total reps around 10. That's 3x3, 5x2, 5–3–2.

- For hypertrophy work, keep the total reps between 15–25. That's 5x5, 3x8, 3x5.

- For hinges, the reps will depend on the movement—do more for kettlebell work like swings, less for deadlifts and the O lifts.

- For loaded carries: Do them.

I don't want to deep dive on this too much, but I'm not a big fan of rotation work in the weightroom. It could be my 50-year career as a thrower; 10,000 throws a year (at least) is probably enough rotation work for me. But, as I hammered this out (HA! I was also a hammer thrower... well, I thought it was funny), I was reminded what I was told by a biomechanist who specializes in throwing: It's not rotation—it's anti-rotation that makes the implements go far.

High-level throwing has been described as driving as fast as you can and smashing into a brick wall. Your head snaps forward and... bad things happen. When we throw, we stop HARD and the implement comes around. When teaching linemen to block, we stress "don't get turned." That's anti-rotation work.

We tend to become asymmetrical, so always let the less strong side dictate the reps. If I can do two presses with the left arm, I just do two with the right. I learned this from Taylor Lewis, an up and coming strength coach: If I keep improving my strong side, the other side will never catch up. It's funny to think of this now, but some of my early articles were about one-arm lifts, and a lot of people thought they were crazy. They have become fairly mainstream now.

STRENGTH TRAINING *LESS THAN 10 REPS* HYPERTROPHY *15–25 REPS*	ANTI-ROTATION WORK
(Bench) Press Pushup	One-Arm Bench Press One-Arm Overhead Press
Pullup Row	One-Arm TRX Row
Reps for Push, Pull and Squat: Same total Double-Kettlebell Front Squat The Whole Squat Family	**Let the "less" strong side determine the reps**
Five sets of two are strength Three sets of eight are hypertrophy	One-Arm Carries: **Suitcase Carry** Waiter Walk Rack Walk

As we move to the right, snaP takes over. We had a discussion not long ago and someone noted that the perfect way to train from kid to casket would be:

Ballistics (Olympic lifts, swings, kettlebell snatches), basic plyometrics

Grinds (powerlifts, general push, pull, hinge, squat)

Hypertrophy (bodybuilding... with mobility)

Or, more succinctly: O lift, then powerlift, then bodybuild.

Ballistic work tends to insist on point, push and snaP without having to use words to explain it.

"Perfect" is always a nice word to use when talking about training, isn't it?

When I look at exercise selection, it really comes down to a discussion of two questions:

Can we do X? Done correctly, yes.

Should we do X? It depends.

If you don't have the equipment, the facilities, the abilities and the time to teach something, I'd argue you probably don't want your people to do it. And, frankly, some people simply don't need to learn every single thing in the buffet of training.

When it comes to athletes, I find exercise selection to be very simple. Now, again, let's review the key to just about everything: I said it would be simple, not easy.

With athletes, I focus on two things in training: snap and work capacity. Snapacity.

Let's look closer:

MOVEMENT	PLANKS AS A PROGRAM	STRENGTH TRAINING *LESS THAN 10 REPS* HYPERTROPHY *15-25 REPS*	ANTI-ROTATION WORK	TRIADS	OLYMPIC LIFTS
PUSH	PUPPs Plank	(Bench) Press Pushup	One-arm Bench Press One-arm Over-head Press		
PULL	Bat Wing	Pullup Row	One-arm RX Row		
HINGE	Glute Bridge with AB Hold	Hip Thrust Rack DLs Goad Bag Swing	Hill Sprints Stadium Steps Skipping Bounding High Knee Work	Push Press/Jerk Swings Litvi/Sprint/LitviSleds	Squat Snatch Clean and Jerk
SQUAT	Goblet Squats 6-point Rocks	Double KB Front Squat The Full Squat Family	Bear Hug Carries Bear Crawls Bear Hug Carries with Monster Walk		
LOADED CARRY	Farmer's Walk Horn Walk	Prowler Car Push	One-arm Carries: Suitcase Carry Waiter Walk Rack Walk		

The two arrows lead us from the hip thrust, rack deadlift and goat bag swing outward toward the two Olympic lifts. We move from simple loaded hinging to more aggressive explosive movements. These build snap.

The outlined boxes are the work capacity movements. Hill sprints revolutionized my coaching in both American football and track and field. They are exhausting, exhilarating and safe. The boxes reflect the best of the movements I found for safely building work capacity. Something as simple as pushing a car for a few blocks might forever change the way you think about training.

My overall training and performance improved when I started doing Highland Games. Later, through the lens of experience, I realized HGs made me refocus snapacity.

The concept of snapacity works well with the traditional method of using the bow and arrow image or Doctor Stu McGill's insight of the hammer and stone.

For the performance athlete, the three Ps knit together constantly in training and competition. Preparation must reflect the needs for a high level of moving planks, great strength and explosive ability (Point, Push, snaP). The coach must have a full toolkit for training both snap and work capacity.

Which, of course, leads to snapacity.

Appendix Nine
The Updated 10,000 Swing Challenge

Recently, I posted a picture of my daughter doing the 10,000 swing challenge. Then someone commented, "You're a little late to the party."

I thought this was odd.

I "invented" the damn thing.

A few years ago, Chris Shugart wanted me to write an article about a kettlebell challenge. At the time, "challenges" had become a thing. People wanted articles that offered a workout or training plan that was difficult but doable.

We settled on a 10,000 swing challenge. But, first… I had to do it.

I NEVER outline a training program in public without doing it first. Ever. I've told you that.

The next morning, Mike Warren Brown and I grabbed two 24-kilogram bells off the rack and got to work. The original plan was a thousand swings a day.

Ten days x 1,000 swings a day = 10,000 swings, right?

Well, not so fast.

First, Mike and I are kettlebell teachers, so we actually SWING the bells with violent hip thrusts and a vertical plank when the bell nears horizontal. Day one, we got our 1,000.

Day two, after we got to 800, I noted an issue: I had lost my ability to feel the back of my body from basically my knees to my neck.

We then decided: Twenty days x 500 swings a day.

And... it worked.

Within weeks, Chris told me that 80,000 forum posts and discussions had exploded the internet. In the past few days, weeks and months, the 10,000 Swing Challenge has reemerged as one of the simplest—and maybe best—home training programs that provide results, a challenge... and doesn't suck.

It's still good. It's still logical.

But many can't do the original. Mike and I have big engines. We know kettlebell swings. We can hold the swinging bells up to 50 reps. I was to discover this is the issue, so over time, I developed other options.

For the record, every time I changed the program, I did 10,000 swings. So, remember this: EVERY option reflects a four-week commitment to testing this... by me and Mike, and many others. Before you raise your hand with a "better" idea, do the workouts as listed.

I offer three new ideas. Remember, the original workout plan is very good, and you might learn some things about mixing swings with hypertrophy.

OPTION ONE: JUST DO IT!

This one is so simple, you might miss the genius: Do 500 swings a day.

Do 500 swings any way you get there. My daughter, Lindsay (state champion in the shot put and a kettlebell instructor), uses this one.

Begin your swings. Go until you get technical issues, grip problems, fatigue or boredom. Stop. Then rest, do mobility work or something else and… go.

Just keep building upon the reps. I announce where I am to the universe every single time I put down the bell just to remember where I am. I have to write the number in my journal too.

Over 10,000 reps, you're going to forget "how many." Trust me.

The reps could look like this:

> 13—the first set starts at one and going to 13
>
> 24—the second set starts at 14 and ends at 24
>
> 40—set three goes longer than the first two sets
>
> 49—perhaps a slippery grip here; put the bell down

Continue to 500, finish the workout, and go home.

Oddly, I get questions about this.

"How many reps per set?"

As many as appropriate.

"How many is that?"

As many as appropriate.

"How many is that?"

This can go on for days.

OPTION TWO: THE WELL-BELLED APPROACH

I like this option a lot if, and only if, you have lots of bells. Line up your bells on the floor. I have 26 total bells, and we have lined up 25 of them—we didn't keep the 4k for obvious reasons—and did 10 reps each… twice.

Boom! Done!

And, honestly, this is a really good way to do the challenge. I recommend not putting them in order—light to heavy or heavy to light. Rather, just have them spaced out in some random pattern. It's actually fun to go from the 48k to a 10k to a 24k.

If you have three, I suggest the order of medium to light to heavy. If you have more bells, generally start and finish each round with medium bells, and place the other options between those.

Now, do some simple math and reflection.

If you don't have any massive bells, do 15 reps with every load. This will add up fast. Every round will be 75 reps if you have five bells.

The upside of this variation is that all you need to remember is the number of rounds. Ten bells and 10 reps means only five rounds. Mentally, that will go by fast.

I guess I under-appreciate how hard the challenge is because I know what's coming up. Day one and day two just aren't that hard. I'm bored by day 17, and it becomes a bit of a mental grind. This option seems the least grinding.

OPTION THREE: ONE-STOP SHOP APPROACH

The original program was very good. Options one and two really work well at easing the mental and physical issues that happen when you block off a month of your calendar and decide to swing 500 times a day five days a week.

This final option can be a program for the rest of your life. Between sets of swings, add a strength exercise or a mobility or flexibility exercise. I use the fundamental human movements: push, pull, hinge, squat, loaded carries.

Since swings are hinges, you can certainly drop the hinge movements, but I like a little variation like rack deadlifts or trap bar deadlifts. Hip thrusts and variations are fine too.

I don't give advice about the number of reps to do between the swings; it really varies. If you wish to just do one exercise (the original program), you'll find you need very few reps per round to really feel it.

I tend to use more one-arm work, and do this variation just to keep things interesting. Let's give a very simple example and programs I use and recommend.

25 swings
One-arm press (left)
25 swings
One-arm press (right)
25 swings
One-arm row (left)
25 swings
One-arm row (right)
25 swings
Deadlift variation
25 swings
Goblet squat
25 swings
Marching in place with load in the left hand (suitcase)
25 swings
Marching in place with load in the right hand (suitcase)
25 swings
Pumps (cobra to downward dog)
25 swings
Repeat

There you go: 500 swings, plus a nice, basic full-body workout.

Let me give you more detailed options. You won't recognize every lift, but I show most of them to you on my Dan John Youtube channel. You can print these workouts using the PDF at:

https://danjohn.net/wp-content/uploads/500-Supp-Groups.pdf

GROUP A

1. *35 swings*
2. *Pushups*
3. *15 swings*
4. *Windmill stick right*
5. *35 swings*
6. *TRX T pull*
7. *15 swings*
8. *Windmill stick left*
9. *35 swings*
10. *Trap bar deadlift*
11. *15 swings*
12. *Stoney stretch, right knee down (RKD)*
13. *35 swings*
14. *Goblet squat*
15. *15 swings*
16. *Stoney stretch, left knee down (LKD)*
17. *35 swings*
18. *Rolling 45s*
19. *15 swings*
20. *Pump—downward dog/cobra*

GROUP B

1. *35 swings*

2. *One-arm press, right arm*

3. *15 swings*

4. *TRX long stretch, right*

5. *35 swings*

6. *One-arm press, left arm*

7. *15 swings*

8. *TRX long stretch, left*

9. *35 swings*

10. *TRX Y pull*

11. *15 swings*

12. *Hip flexor stretch (RKD)*

13. *35 swings*

14. *Goblet squat*

15. *15 swings*

16. *Hip flexor stretch (LKD)*

17. *35 swings*

18. *Rolling 45 Ts*

19. *15 swings*

20. *March in place*

GROUP C

1. 35 swings
2. Military press with a barbell
3. 15 swings
4. TRX cossack stretch , right leg squat (RLS)
5. 35 swings
6. TRX double row
7. 15 swings
8. TRX cossack stretch, left leg squat (LLS)
9. 35 swings
10. Flying bird dog, right foot down (RFD)
11. 15 swings
12. Six-point rock
13. 35 swings
14. Flying bird dog, left foot down (LFD)
15. 15 swings
16. Six-point neck nod
17. 35 swings
18. Double kettlebell front squat
19. 15 swings
20. Deep TRX squat hang

GROUP D

1. *35 swings*
2. *Double kettlebell press*
3. *15 swings*
4. *Six-point Zenith right*
5. *35 swings*
6. *TRX single-arm row, right hand*
7. *15 swings*
8. *Six point Zenith left*
9. *35 swings*
10. *TRX single-arm row, left hand*
11. *15 swings*
12. *Wrist vents*
13. *35 swings*
14. *Barbell front squat*
15. *15 swings*
16. *Reverse wrist vents*
17. *35 swings*
18. *Bulgarian goat bag swing*
19. *15 swings*
20. *Basic foot vent*

GROUP E

1. *35 swings*
2. *TRX pushup*
3. *15 swings*
4. *TRX single-arm rainbow, right side*
5. *35 swings*
6. *TRX pushup*
7. *15 swings*
8. *TRX single-arm rainbow, left side*
9. *35 swings*
10. *Romanian deadlift with a kettlebell*
11. *15 swings*
12. *Six-point rock*
13. *35 swings*
14. *Goblet squat*
15. *15 swings*
16. *Thick bar pullups*
17. *35 swings*
18. *Dead bugs*
19. *15 swings*
20. *Ring pullups*

GROUP F

1. *35 swings*
2. *French press*
3. *15 swings*
4. *Curl*
5. *35 swings*
6. *TRX triceps extension*
7. *15 swings*
8. *TRX biceps curl*
9. *35 swings*
10. *Mini-band walk, right*
11. *15 swings*
12. *Mini-band walk, left*
13. *35 swings*
14. *Hip rip, right*
15. *15 swings*
16. *Hip rip, left*
17. *35 swings*
18. *Getup, right hand loaded*
19. *15 swings*
20. *Getup, left hand loaded*

Again, use your own variations and movements as appropriate.

I like to pick two different groups when we do 500 reps (each group has 250 swing reps), but a few of the variations work well going back to back. The best might be Group A for repeating, but your mileage may vary.

As when you first learned the goblet squat, the slosh pipe, the waiter and suitcase carry, I tend to be "late to the party."

After I came up with the ideas.

Appendix Ten
The Original 10,000 Swing Program

Without challenges, the human body will soften. We thrive when we push our boundaries, reach goals and blast personal records. We perform better, we look better and we feel alive.

Get this straight: We're either progressing or regressing. There is no "maintenance phase." Moderation in training can easily turn into stagnation. And moderation is for sissies. If we want to improve, we have to seek new challenges, struggle and win.

The 10,000 swing kettlebell workout is just such a challenge. And… it will rapidly transform your body in only four weeks.

I don't write training programs by reading textbooks and studies. I create them in the field, deep in the trenches with real athletes and people whose lives literally depend on their physical abilities.

To create and refine this program, 18 other coaches and athletes and I met several days every week to put it to the test. Here's what we experienced:

- Everyone got leaner, dropping a waist size or two in 20 workouts.

- Every person made visual muscular improvements in their physiques, adding lean body mass.

- Every lifter increased grip strength and greatly increased work capacity and athletic conditioning. We could all train longer and harder when we went back to our normal training programs.

- After the program, every lifter saw a noted improvement in the core lifts. PRs fell like dominos. Full-body strength and power shot through the roof.

- Abs were more visible. Glute strength was tremendously better. The abs and glutes discovered how to work again, leading to athletic improvements in sports and in the weight room.

Here's how to do it. In four or five weeks, you're going to perform 10,000 proper kettlebell swings. These will be split among 20 workouts. You'll do 500 swings per workout.

Between sets of swings, you'll perform low-volume, basic strength exercises. You will train four or five days per week. Train two days on, one day off, and repeat. Men will use a 24kg kettlebell (53 pounds). Women will use 16kg (35 pounds).

This is a stand-alone program. If you feel you're able to do a second workout during the same day, it means you're "under-belled." You're either not going heavy enough or not training with maximal effort.

THE SWINGS: CLUSTERS, SETS, AND REPS

Use an undulating rep scheme to reach 500 total reps per workout.

Set One: 10 reps

Set Two: 15 reps

Set Three: 25 reps

Set Four: 50 reps

You've now completed 100 reps—one cluster. Repeat the cluster four more times for a total of 500 swings. Between sets, experienced lifters will add a low-volume strength movement.

THE STRENGTH MOVEMENTS

Use a strength movement with low volume between sets of swings. The best exercises are:

Press (barbell overhead press or one-arm press)

Dip

Goblet squat

Chinup

Other acceptable choices: front squat, pistol squat, handstand pushup, wide-grip loaded pullup and the muscle-up. Use a 1–2–3 rep scheme for most movements.

Here's an example using the press:

10 swings

Press one rep

15 swings

Press two reps

25 swings

Press three reps

50 swings

Rest 30–60 seconds

For the 1–2–3 lifts, use your five-rep max weight.

For the dip, you'll need more reps. Use a 2–3–5 rep scheme.

If you choose to do the program five days per week, on one of those days you'll only do the swings, leaving out the strength work between rounds. If you train four days per week, you'll use the strength movements every workout.

You might decide to use a different strength movement every workout, rotating between the press, dip, goblet squat, and chinup. I also like using two days of chinups and two days of presses.

Remember, choose only one strength movement per workout.

REST PERIODS

After each round of 10, 15, and 25 reps, rest 30–60 seconds. The first cluster will be easy and you can jam through it. In the later clusters, you'll need the full 60 seconds or more for grip recovery.

After each set of 50, the rest will extend to three or more minutes. During this post-50 rest period, perform a corrective. Stretch anything that needs it, such as the hip flexors. Do a mobility movement of choice.

PROGRESSION

Time your workouts. Each week you should be getting faster. Your time in workout #20 should clobber your time in the first workout. For the strength lifts, the goal is to use a weight that's challenging on the first workout and easy by the last.

Here's what the program looks like for most lifters:

SAMPLE PROGRAM

Day One

10 swings

Press one rep

15 swings

Press two reps

25 swings

Press three reps

50 swings

Rest 30–60 seconds; repeat four more times.

By the end of the workout, you'll have completed 500 swings and 30 presses.

Day Two

10 swings

Dip two reps

15 swings

Dip three reps

25 swings

Dip five reps

50 swings

Rest 30–60 seconds; repeat four more times.

By the end of the workout, you'll have completed 500 swings and 50 dips. Remember, for dips you're using a 2–3–5 rep scheme, not 1–2–3 as you do in other lifts.

Day Three

Off

Day Four

10 swings

Goblet squat one rep

15 swings

Goblet squat two reps

25 swings

Goblet squat three reps

50 swings

Rest 30–60 seconds; repeat four more times.

By the end of the workout, you'll have completed 500 swings and 30 goblet squats.

Day Five

10 swings

Chinup one rep

15 swings

Chinup two reps

25 swings

Chinup three reps

50 swings

Rest 30–60 seconds; repeat four more times.

By the end of the workout, you'll have completed 500 swings and 30 chinups.

Day Six

Off

Day Seven

Off or begin the cycle again

If you begin the cycle again because you want to use the program five days a week, remember to do only the swings during one workout each week.

SWING TECHNIQUE

The swing is a hip hinge. Basically, it's the position you take in a standing long jump. Look for maximum hip bend and minimal knee bend. It's not a squat.

Begin in the "silverback gorilla" position. Slide the kettlebell back a bit and vigorously hike the bell at your zipper. Hinge deeply, and let the forearms slide through the thighs. Then, snap up to a vertical plank position.

There is no start or finish to a correct swing. The vertical plank is a moment to grab the bell and toss it back to the zipper. The hinge causes a rebound, and we pop back to a plank.

Ensure the following: glutes clenched, lats connected to the shoulders, arms snapped directly in front of the body. Don't let the kettlebell float much higher—grab it and toss it back to your zipper. The kettlebell should not be brought overhead.

The swing should be aggressive, explosive and attacked with a high tempo.

Finally, if you do this, congratulate yourself for actually finishing a program. That's rare in today's world.

You're now in extraordinarily better shape than you were four or five weeks ago. Your training should be poised to take off. I recommend putting these newfound abilities to work with a basic strength template, such as Jim Wendler's 5/3/1.

Index

About the Author

If you ever get to spend time with Dan John, consider yourself lucky. You'll laugh, you'll cry...and well, you'll probably talk about your gut biome more than once. If Dan (I call him "Dad") asks for sauerkraut on the side of his meal, go with it! Don't ask questions.

One thing you'll notice in your time together is that he has a quote for everything. And I mean everything.

"Last throw, best throw."

"You're not good enough to be frustrated."

"I've got that bad knee..."

"It's not where you start; it's where you finish."

Why does he love his quotes so much?

Not sure, but I have my theories. I never met my grandparents, but have heard enough to know they were... uh, straight to the point. Not a lot of fluff from good ole Al and Aileen.

As my friend Kevin from *The Office* says, "Why waste time say lot word when few word do trick?"

Quotes—they're straight to the point, easy to remember.

When you have athletes feeling defeated, they're not going to listen to the full explanation: "Well, Mark, see, it takes 10,000 hours to become great at something..."

No, no, no. From Dan, it's, "Mark, you aren't good enough to be frustrated."

"Life is about choices."

After a night of drinking, Dad usually delivers this line to me with a snicker. "Yes, yes, I KNOW," I'll throw back at him and promptly ask for some Advil.

I've heard that line on repeat for years. Well, I guess "heard" should be in quotation marks because even though I "heard" it a million times, I never internalized it. Every time he said it, I thought he was insinuating that I'd made a wrong choice.

But he wasn't.

For Dan, there's no such thing as a "bad" or "good" choice, a "right" or "wrong" choice. For him, it's merely to remind you the choice you make today will impact your tomorrow. Or in a week. Or in three years.

From what you eat to whom you'll marry, those are all choices we have to make.

It seems heavy, but don't fear. Life... well, it's about choices. Approach each decision with the mindset of, "How will this affect me today? How about tomorrow?"

I mean...isn't that what Dan John would do?

Lindsay John

Made in the USA
Coppell, TX
13 January 2022

71525532R10168